From Exiles
to Immigrants

THE ASIAN AMERICAN EXPERIENCE

From Exiles to Immigrants

THE REFUGEES FROM SOUTHEAST ASIA

Ronald Takaki

PROFESSOR OF ETHNIC STUDIES
THE UNIVERSITY OF CALIFORNIA AT BERKELEY

Adapted by Rebecca Stefoff

WITH CAROL TAKAKI

Chelsea House Publishers

New York ✳ Philadelphia

On the cover: A group of Southeast Asian refugees arrive by boat
in the Philippines in 1979.

Chelsea House Publishers

EDITORIAL DIRECTOR Richard Rennert
EXECUTIVE MANAGING EDITOR Karyn Gullen Browne
COPY CHIEF Robin James
PICTURE EDITOR Adrian G. Allen
CREATIVE DIRECTOR Robert Mitchell
ART DIRECTOR Joan Ferrigno
PRODUCTION MANAGER Sallye Scott

The Asian American Experience

SENIOR EDITOR Jake Goldberg
SERIES DESIGN Marjorie Zaum

Staff for *From Exiles to Immigrants*
EDITORIAL ASSISTANT Scott D. Briggs
PICTURE RESEARCHER Pat Burns

Library of Congress Cataloging-in-Publication Data
Takaki, Ronald T.

From exiles to immigrants: the refugees from southeast
Asia/Ronald Takaki.
        p. cm. — (The Asian American experience)
        Includes bibliographical references and index.
ISBN 0-7910-2185-8
1. Indochinese Americans—Juvenile literature. 2. Immigrants—
United States—Juvenile literature. 3. United States—Emigration
and immigration—Juvenile literature. 4. Asia, Southeastern—
Emigration and immigration—Juvenile literature. I. Title. II. Series:
Asian American experience (New York, N.Y.)
E184.I43T35 1995   94–37529
973'.049922—dc20   CIP
                                                    AC

Contents

An ethnic Chinese woman from Vietnam, one of thousands of refugees who sought sanctuary in Hong Kong in 1987, cradles her child while waiting to be admitted to a processing center.

From a Different Shore

AS A CHILD IN HAWAII, I GREW UP IN A MULTICULTURAL corner of America. My own family had roots in Japan and China.

Grandfather Kasuke Okawa arrived in Hawaii in 1866, and my father, Toshio Takaki, came as a 13-year-old boy in 1918. My stepfather, Koon Keu Young, sailed from China to the islands when he was a teenager.

My neighbors were Japanese, Chinese, Hawaiian, Filipino, Portuguese, and Korean. Behind my house, Alice Liu and her friends played the traditional Chinese game of mahjongg late into the night, the clicking of the tiles lulling me to sleep.

Next to us the Miuras flew billowing and colorful carp kites on Japanese boy's day. I heard voices with different accents, different languages, and saw children of different colors.

Together we went barefoot to school and played games like baseball and *jan ken po*. We spoke "pidgin English," a melodious language of the streets and community. "Hey, da kind tako ono, you know," we would say, combining English, Japanese, and Hawaiian. "This octopus is delicious." Racially and culturally diverse, we all thought of ourselves as Americans.

But we did not know why families representing such an array of nationalities from different shores were living together and sharing their cultures and a common language. Our teachers and textbooks did not explain the diversity of our community or the sources of our unity.

After graduation from high school, I attended a college in a midwestern town where I found myself invited to "dinners for foreign students" sponsored by local churches and clubs like the Rotary. I politely tried to explain to my kind hosts that I was not a "foreign student." My fellow students and even my professors would ask me how long I had been in America and where I had learned to speak English. "In this country," I would reply. And sometimes I would add: "I was born in America, and my family has been here for three generations."

Asian Americans have been here for over 150 years. They are diverse, coming originally from countries such as China, Japan, Korea, the Philippines, India, Vietnam, Laos, and Cambodia. Many of them live in Chinatowns, the colorful streets filled with sidewalk vegetable stands and crowds of people carrying shopping bags; their communities are also called Little Tokyo, Koreatown, and Little Saigon. Asian Americans work in hot kitchens and bus tables in restaurants with elegant names like Jade Pagoda and Bombay Spice. In garment factories, Chinese and Korean women hunch over whirling sewing machines, their babies sleeping nearby on blankets. In the Silicon Valley of California, rows and rows of Vietnamese and Laotian women serve as the eyes and hands of production assembly lines for computer chip industries. Tough Chinese gang members strut on Grant Avenue in San Francisco and Canal Street in New York's Chinatown. In La Crosse, Wisconsin, Hmong refugees from Laos, now dependent on welfare, sit and stare at the snowdrifts outside their windows. Asian American engineers do complex research in the laboratories of the high-technology industries along

Route 128 in Massachusetts. Asian Americans seem to be everywhere on university campuses.

Today, Asian Americans belong to the fastest growing ethnic group in the United States. Kept out of the United States by immigration restriction laws in the 19th and early 20th centuries, Asians have recently been coming again to America. The 1965 immigration act reopened the gates to immigrants from Asia, allowing 20,000 immigrants from each country to enter every year. In the early 1990s, half of all immigrants entering annually are Asian.

The growth of the Asian American population has been dramatic: In 1960, there were only 877,934 Asians in the United States, representing a mere one-half of 1% of the American people. Thirty years later, they numbered about seven million, or 3% of the population. They included 1,645,000 Chinese, 1,400,000 Filipinos, 845,000 Japanese, 815,000 Asian Indians, 800,000 Koreans, 614,000 Vietnamese, 150,000 Laotians, 147,000 Cambodians, and 90,000 Hmong. By the year 2000, Asian Americans will probably represent 4% of the total United States population. In California, Asian Americans already make up 10% of the state's inhabitants, compared with 7.5% for African Americans.

Yet very little is known about Asian Americans and their history. Many existing history books give Asian Americans only passing notice—or overlook them entirely. "When one hears Americans tell of the immigrants who built this nation," Congressman Norman Mineta of California observed, "one is often led to believe that all our forebears came from Europe. When one hears stories about the pioneers going West to shape the land, the Asian immigrant is rarely mentioned."

Indeed, many history books have equated "American" with "white" or "European" in origin. In his prize-winning study, *The Uprooted*, Harvard historian Oscar Handlin presented—to use the book's subtitle—"the Epic Story of the Great Migrations that Made the American People." But Handlin's "epic story" completely left out the "uprooted" from lands across the Pacific Ocean and the "great migrations" from Asia that also helped to make "the American people." As Americans, we have origins in Europe, the Americas, Africa, and also Asia.

We need to include Asians in the history of America. How and why, we ask in this series, were the experiences of these various groups—Chinese, Japanese, Korean, Filipino, Asian Indian, and Southeast Asian—similar to and different from each other? Comparing the experiences of different nationalities can help us see what events were particular to a group and also highlight the experiences they all shared.

Why did Asian immigrants leave everything they knew and loved to come to a strange world so far away? They were "pushed" by hardships in the homelands and "pulled" by demands for their labor in Canada, Brazil, and especially the United States. But what were their own fierce dreams— from the first enterprising Chinese miners of the 1850s in search of "Gold Mountain" to the recent refugees fleeing frantically on helicopters and leaking boats from the ravages of war in Vietnam?

Besides their points of origin, we need to examine the experiences of Asian Americans in different geographical regions, especially Hawaii compared with the mainland. The time of arrival also shaped their lives and communities. About one million people entered the United States between the California gold rush of 1849 and the 1924 immigration act that cut off the flow of peoples from Asian countries. After a break of some 40 years, a second group numbering about four million came between 1965 and 1990. How do we compare the two waves of Asian immigration?

To answer our questions in these volumes, we must study Asian Americans as men and women with minds, wills, and voices. By "voices" we mean their own words and stories as told in their oral histories, conversations, speeches, and songs as well as their own writings—diaries, letters, newspapers, novels, and poems. We need to know the ordinary people.

So much of history has been the story of kings and elites, as if the "little people" were invisible and voiceless. An Asian American told an interviewer: "I am a second-generation Korean American without any achievements in life and I have no education. What is it you want to hear from me? My life is not worth telling to anyone." Similarly, a Chinese immigrant said: "You know, it seems to me there's no use in me telling you all this! I was just a simple worker, a farm worker around here. My story is not going to interest anybody." But others realize they are worthy of attention. "What is it you want to know?" an old Filipino immigrant asked a researcher. "Talk about history. What's that . . . ah, the story of my life . . . and how people lived with each other in my time."

Their stories can enable us to understand Asians as actors in the making of history and as people entitled to dignity. "I hope this survey do a lot of good for Chinese people," a Chinese man told an interviewer from Stanford University in the 1920s. "Make American people realize that Chinese people are humans. I think very few American people really know anything about Chinese." Elderly Asians want the younger generations to know about their experiences. "Our stories should be listened to by many young people," said a 91-year-old retired Japanese plantation laborer. "It's for their sake. We really had a hard time, you know."

The stories of Asian immigrations belong to our country's history. They need to be recorded in our history books, for they reflect the making of America as a nation of immigrants, as a place where men and women came to find a new beginning. At first, many Asian immigrants—probably most of them—saw themselves as sojourners, or temporary migrants. Like many European immigrants such as the Italians and Greeks, they came to America thinking they would be here only a short time. They had left their wives and children behind in their homelands. Their plan was to work here for a few years and then return home with money. But, after their arrival, many found themselves staying. They became settlers instead of remaining sojourners. Bringing their families to their adopted country, they began putting down new roots in America.

But, coming here from Asia, many of America's immigrants found they were not allowed to feel at home in the United States. Even their grandchildren and great-grandchildren still find they are not viewed and accepted as Americans. "We feel that we're a guest in someone else's house," said third generation Ron Wakabayashi, National Director of the Japanese American Citizens League, "that we can never really relax and put our feet on the table."

Behind Wakabayashi's complaint is the question: Why have Asian Americans been considered outsiders? America's immigrants from Pacific shores found they were forced to remain strangers in the new land. Their experiences here were profoundly different from the experiences of European immigrants. Asian immigrants had qualities they could not change or hide—the shape of their eyes, the color of their hair, the complexion of their skin. They were subjected not only to cultural and ethnic prejudice but also to racism. Unlike the Irish and other groups from Europe, Asian immigrants were not treated as individuals but as members of a group with distinctive physical characteristics. Regardless of their personal merits, they sadly discovered, they could not gain acceptance in the larger society.

Unlike European immigrants, Asians were victimized by laws and policies that discriminated on the basis of race. The Chinese Exclusion Act of 1882 barred the Chinese from coming to America because they were Chinese. The National Origins Act of 1924 totally prohibited Japanese immigration.

The laws determined not only who could come to America but also who could become citizens. Decades before Asian immigration began, the United States had already defined the complexion of its citizens: the Naturalization Law of 1790 had specified that naturalized citizenship was to be reserved for "whites." This law remained in effect until 1952. Unlike white ethnic immigrants from countries like Ireland, Asian immigrants were denied citizenship and also the right to vote.

But America also had an opposing tradition and vision, springing from the reality of racial and cultural "diversity." Ours has been, as Walt Whitman celebrated so lyrically, "a teeming Nation of nations" composed of a "vast, surging, hopeful army of workers," a new society where all should be welcomed, "Chinese, Irish, German,—all, all, without exceptions." In the early 20th century, a Japanese immigrant described in poetry a lesson that had been learned by farm laborers of different nationalities—Japanese, Filipino, Mexican, and Asian Indian:

> *People harvesting*
> *Work together unaware*
> *Of racial problems.*

A Filipino immigrant laborer in California expressed a similar hope and understanding. America was, Macario Bulosan told his brother Carlos, "not a land of one race or one class of men" but "a new world" of respect and unconditional opportunities for all who toiled and suffered from oppression, from "the first Indian that offered peace in Manhattan to the last Filipino pea pickers." Asian immigrants came here, as one of them expressed it, searching for "a door into America" and seeking "to build a new life with untried materials." He asked: "Would it be possible for an immigrant like me to become a part of the American dream?"

This series invites students to learn how Asian Americans belong to the larger story of the rich multicultural mosaic called the United States of America.

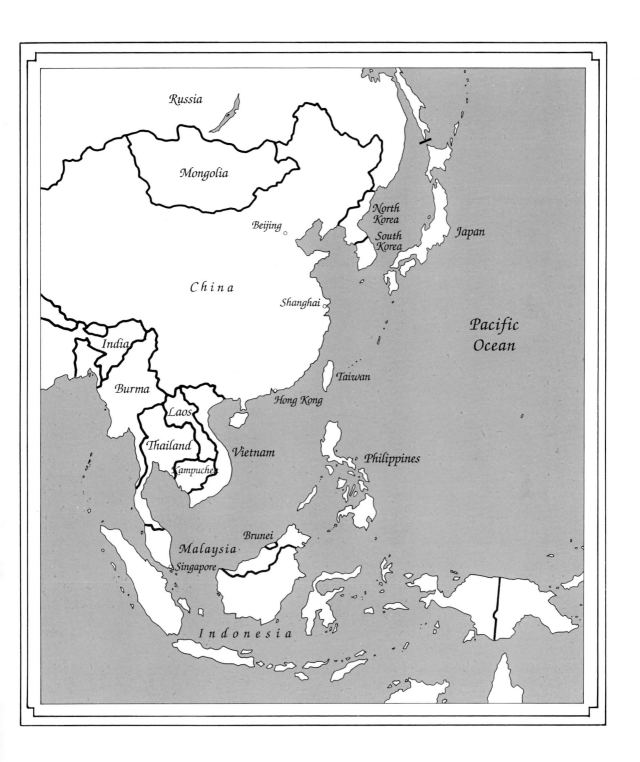

The first wave of Vietnamese refugees arrived in the United States in the late 1970s, fleeing the communist regime that had taken control of the former South Vietnam. They were the vanguard of the Southeast Asian community in America.

Chapter One

The Refugees

IN SEPTEMBER 1979, A TEENAGE GIRL NAMED LAMTHIANE Inthirath arrived in Massachusetts with her family. They had come from Laos, a country in Southeast Asia, and they had never been far from home before. Inthirath and her family had not come to the United States for a visit or a vacation—they had come to live in America. "I did not know any English when I first came here," she later recalled. "I was very frightened for myself and my family. Moving into a different country and environment is not easy for anybody."

Inthirath recalled that her family had "many problems and difficulties as newcomers." One of the biggest problems was communication, for they did not know how to speak English. The Inthirath family was being looked after by Americans who acted as their sponsors, helping them to adjust to American life, but the sponsors did not speak Lao or Thai, the Southeast Asian languages spoken by the Inthiraths. "I could not even tell them that I was sick from the airplane," said Inthirath of her arrival in her new country.

The United States confronted Inthirath and her family with what she called "culture shock." Getting used to the food in their new home was not easy. "We had never eaten American food before and we did not know how to eat it," Inthirath said. "My grandmother who was sixty at that time especially had difficulties; she refused to touch anything for quite some time."

Some of Inthirath's most challenging moments came during her second week in America, when she started eighth grade at a local school. She remembered getting up early that morning and dressing in her best clothes. "I was full of excitement to meet more people," she said, "but deep down inside I felt afraid of something." Inthirath was the only

Southeast Asian student in her school. "[I felt] uneasy and frustated when I could not speak English." Other students would ask her name and where she had come from, but she did not know how to answer them—and then, she recalled, they laughed at her. "I wanted so much to express myself and tell them who I was," Inthirath later said. "I think almost every newcomer experiences the communication gap."

Inthirath studied hard to learn English so that she would not remain isolated from the other kids, but still some of her classmates did not accept her. During her freshman year in high school, she had trouble with a group of boys who laughed at her and threw cookies at her. Because they thought she was Chinese, they insulted her with racist terms such as "chink." This treatment continued for weeks and Inthirath's anger grew, until one day in study hall she could not swallow their insults any longer:

> *I realized that I was different, but I did not expect other students to treat me like that. My frustration built up and I came to the point where I had to do something about it. I had to stand up for myself; if I did not nobody would. I knew the consequences, however I preferred to end the ridiculing right then rather than have them carry it on. I got up rapidly without giving the boys a chance to move from their seats. I threw my math book in one boy's face. I woke up the whole classroom. The teacher asked what I was doing. I told him exactly what had happened. I thought he was going to send me to the office for detention, but he did not. Instead, he sent those boys down and they got two days after-school detention.*

The confrontation brought about a change for the better, added Inthirath. "After two detentions they realized I had the

Vietnamese refugees arriving in the United States in 1975. Most of the early refugees were members of the South Vietnamese military or government and their families.

same feelings as others, they made an apology and it was accepted. Shortly we became friends."

Other young Southeast Asians living in the United States have also experienced conflict with Americans, and some of these clashes have been tragic. A boy named Trung came to the United States from Vietnam at the age of 16. Not long after his arrival, he was attacked by four young men while walking home from high school. They surrounded him and yelled, "Get out of America!" and "You are a dog!"

Trung did not want to fight. He simply said, "Okay, okay" and tried to keep walking. Then the four youths pulled out knives. In the fight that followed, the Vietnamese boy was stabbed in the head. "Then I ran," he said later, "with the blood streaming down, and three of them ran after me. Suddenly an old white man came out of his home. 'Hey, man, stop fighting,' he said. 'There's too many people against one.'" The old man helped Trung clean up the blood and called the police, who took Trung to the hospital. "There was much bleeding," Trung recalled. "I felt the hurt after the fighting, and then I felt scared. . . . I did feel angry after the fight, but I am not angry now. When it first happened, I said, 'I want revenge.' But I don't want revenge now. It's a foolish thing."

Trung spoke sadly of feeling like a stranger and an outcast in America, far from his homeland and the family that had remained in Vietnam. His English was poor, and he was able to express himself only in poetry, written in his native language according to the strict rules that govern traditional Vietnamese poetry. Translated into English, Trung's poems reveal his great loneliness:

> *With grief, I see months and days passing,*
> *I miss you, O Vietnam, where repose generations of my*
>   *ancestors.*
> *I miss my small village stretching out amidst the ocean.*
> *Where is my family now? I wonder,*
> *And the old school, when the classes begin,*
> *Are the doe-eyed children still there or already gone?*
> *O my homeland! Why are you still far away from me?*

Horng Kouch came to the United States from Cambodia, another Southeast Asian nation. She arrived in 1980 at the age of 11. Her family, like the Inthirath family from Laos, ended up settling in Massachusetts. And like Lamthiane Inthirath, Kouch experienced a lot of "culture shock" in her new home. Her inability to speak English created a barrier between her and the Americans around her, especially at school. Some of her fellow students laughed at her; most of them ignored her. Later, Kouch was able to look back on these experiences with understanding, saying, "They acted like that because I was different, I came from another country, spoke broken English and looked different." She was, she said, "like a person from another planet."

Despite the language barrier, Kouch and her family managed to cling to some familiar reminders of their home in Cambodia. They wanted to eat Cambodian foods as they were accustomed to do, but they could not communicate their needs to their sponsors. Finally, they used a dictionary to explain that they needed rice, chopsticks, and soy sauce. The United States was full of surprises. One surprise was snow, which Kouch had never seen before: "It was weird and strange to see white dirt on the ground. And the weather was so cold; we had never felt so cold before. . . . For the first few months we all had colds because we didn't know how to dress warmly enough, although now we are used to it." Kouch was also surprised to see teenagers holding hands in the streets, and even kissing in public—behavior almost never seen in Cambodia. Such sights made it clear to Kouch that she had truly entered a new and different world.

After a year in the United States, Kouch was placed in the seventh grade in a junior high school, taking classes in a program called English as a Second Language, or ESL. By the next year, her English had improved so much that she was able to leave the ESL program and start attending regular classes, where she made the honor roll. After Kouch graduated from high school, she went on to college at the University of

Massachusetts. Her goal was to be "a successful career woman." She hoped to find a career in which she could help other Southeast Asians adjust to their often confusing new lives in the United States.

People from Southeast Asia began coming to North America in large numbers in 1975. By 1985, there were 875,000 Southeast Asians living in the United States and another 50,000 in Canada. By 1994, the Southeast Asian population in the United States was estimated at about 1 million.

The Southeast Asians are the most recent wave of immigrants to cross the Pacific Ocean from Asia. Since the middle of the 19th century, Asians have been coming to North

A newly arrived Vietnamese family with their sponsors in Florida. The sponsors—usually assigned by religious or aid groups—served to ease the transition of the Southeast Asians into their new homes.

America. The first to arrive were Chinese. Over the years, they were followed by Japanese, Korean, Filipino, and Asian Indian immigrants. Many of these Asian immigrants had planned to stay in America only for a short while, to work and save money before returning to their homelands. Some did return, but many settled in America, laying the foundation for today's diverse and ever-growing Asian American population.

Other Asian immigrants have experienced many of the same challenges that confronted the Southeast Asians. Like Lamthiane Inthirath, who felt a sense of "culture shock" when she arrived in Massachusetts from Laos, newcomers from China, Japan, Korea, the Philippines, and India have had to cope with unfamiliar and bewildering sights, sounds, and tastes. They have had to learn a new language and get used to a new climate. And most of them have felt the sting of racial insults and the loneliness of feeling like an outsider.

Yet there is one vitally important difference between the Southeast Asians and nearly all of the other Asians who have come to North America. Generally, the other Asians were immigrants. They came to America for a variety of reasons: some were seeking jobs or opportunities to make money; others wanted to live in an open, democratic society. They experienced economic hardships and political problems that made life difficult in their homelands, so they made the choice to cross the sea to America. They shared the rituals of preparation: gathering money to pay for their passage, packing their most treasured possessions to carry with them on the journey, saying goodbye to family and friends, and thinking and talking about what their new life would be like. A Japanese immigrant of the late 19th century summed up the immigrants' hopeful dreams in a poem:

Huge dreams of fortune
Go with me to foreign lands,
Across the ocean.

The immigrants from Asia traveled across the sea in search of their dreams. But the Southeast Asians were not following dreams—they were fleeing from nightmares. They did not choose to leave their homes; they were driven from their homes by vast, destructive forces. They were refugees, not immigrants. Desperately seeking safety beyond the borders of their own countries, many of these refugees had to leave their homes at a moment's notice, with no time for preparation. Sometimes they fled with no destination in mind. They did not know where they would eventually find themselves.

Most of the immigrants from China, Japan, and other Asian nations could have returned to their homelands if they had wanted to do so. But the Southeast Asian refugees left home with great uncertainty, not knowing whether they would ever be able to return. Many feared that they would never see their homes again. As refugees, they bore a double burden: in addition to the stress of getting used to life in a new country, they were haunted by a sense of permanent separation from everything that was familiar. "Being a refugee," wrote Lucy Nguyen-Hong-Nhiem, who fled to the United States from Vietnam, "means knowing that you will never go home." Many of the Southeast Asian refugees never stopped longing for the homes they unwillingly left behind.

What could drive so many people away from their homes and turn them into refugees? The answer lies in the recent history of Southeast Asia, torn by war and revolution.

Southeast Asia is a region that stretches from Myanmar (once called Burma) in the west to the Philippines in the east. It includes the large nations of Malaysia, Indonesia, and Thailand as well as the much smaller ones of Brunei and Singapore. It also includes the three neighboring countries of Laos, Cambodia, and Vietnam. Along with Thailand, these three countries occupy a peninsula that juts south from China.

Because Laos, Cambodia, and Vietnam are located midway between two large and influential countries, India and China, they have sometimes been grouped together under the name "Indochina." In ancient times, the Laotian, Cambodian,

An elderly Vietnamese woman is overcome with emotion during a Buddhist service at Camp Pendleton near San Clemente, California, as she waits to be released from the refugee camp known as "Camp Talega."

Hue Vo hugs his eight-year-old daughter upon her arrival in Houston. He, his wife, and their three older children had fled Vietnam eight years earlier, leaving their newborn daughter behind. Many Southeast Asian families were ripped apart during the Vietnam War and the years that followed; many have not yet been reunited.

26

and Vietnamese cultures were shaped by traders, missionaries, and conquerors from both India and China. Buddhism traveled from India to Indochina, where it became established as the dominant religion. The Chinese influence was strongest in Vietnam, which at several times was ruled by China. People of Chinese ancestry settled in parts of Vietnam. Cambodia, too, numbered among its population many Chinese.

In the 19th century, the European powers were competing for influence and setting up colonies throughout Africa and Asia. France established control of Vietnam in the 1860s. In the decades that followed, French influence reached into

Laos and Cambodia as well. Together, the three countries were known as French Indochina. They remained under French control for nearly a century.

During World War II (1939–45), the Vietnamese Communist party under the leadership of Ho Chi Minh began fighting the French to regain their country's independence. This conflict ended in 1954. The French and the Vietnamese Communists agreed to divide Vietnam temporarily into two parts, North and South Vietnam. The Communists, who controlled North Vietnam, believed that a nationwide election would soon establish a new government that would reunite the two parts. Instead, a new government was formed in South Vietnam, with the support of the United States, to counter Communist North Vietnam, which was backed by China and the Soviet Union (now Russia). The split between North and South Vietnam was supposed to last only for a short time, but the nationwide election was never held, and civil war erupted.

In the early 1960s, President John F. Kennedy sent U.S. forces to Vietnam. This was the start of American involvement in the Vietnam War. The United States began withdrawing from the war in the early 1970s. The war ended in April 1975, when the government of South Vietnam collapsed and the troops of North Vietnam entered Saigon, the South Vietnamese capital. During the last days of South Vietnam, thousands of people fled to the United States to escape the Communist takeover. They were the first of several waves of Southeast Asian refugees.

A Vietnamese man scrambles aboard the U.S. Navy vessel White Plains, *his only possessions in a bag clutched in his teeth. The* White Plains *rescued him and 28 others in the South China Sea in 1979.*

IMMIGRANTS FROM MANY COUNTRIES HAVE ENDURED hardships during their journeys to America. The refugees from Southeast Asia, however, faced more than the ordinary trials and discomforts of immigrant travel. Their journeys were made in mortal danger, often in secrecy. Many perished on the way; in some cases, families were torn apart, and children saw their parents killed before their eyes. The refugees' journey to America was truly a perilous passage.

Most of the first wave of Vietnamese refugees were U.S. allies—members of the South Vietnamese military or government. When it became clear that North Vietnam was going to win the war, these South Vietnamese officials were desperate to get themselves and their families out of Saigon before the Communists arrived. The United States offered them sanctuary and transported many out of the country in airplanes and helicopters. A week before the collapse of the South Vietnamese government in April 1975, 10,000 to 15,000 people were evacuated from South Vietnam. Then, in the frenzied last days of April, 86,000 Vietnamese were airlifted out of the besieged country. "That morning, April 29," said Nguyen Cao Ky, the last premier of South Vietnam, describing his final hours in Saigon, "I found myself alone at the big headquarters of the general staff. . . . At noontime, all the American helicopters came in for the final, big evacuation. On the ground, there were hundreds of thousands of Vietnamese running—right, left, every way, to find a way to escape. My bodyguards said to me, 'Well, General, it's time for us to go, too.' "

Panic gripped the people. "On those last days of April," remembered a refugee, "[there was] a lot of gunfire and bombing around the capital. People were running on chaotic streets. We got scared. . . . We went to an American building where a lot of Americans and their Vietnamese associates were ready to be picked up by American helicopters." They could "feel" the bombing. "Our houses were shaking," said Thai Dang. "Then afterwards we went outside and saw abandoned guns and army uniforms on the streets. The soldiers in flight had thrown away their weapons and taken off their uniforms [so that the North Vietnamese would not recognize them as enemy troops]. Here and there we saw bodies."

The city shuddered under relentless missile bombardments. Homes and buildings were burning everywhere.

> *Fires spring up like dragon's teeth*
> *At the standpoints of the universe:*
> *A furious, acrid wind sweeps them toward us from all sides;*
> *All around, the horizon burns with the color of death.*

Frightened people rushed to get out of Saigon. From the roof of the American embassy, hundreds climbed frantically onto helicopters. Others drove to the airport, where they abandoned their cars with notes on the windshields: "For those who are left behind." Terrifying images were seared into the refugees' memories. One woman never forgot the sight of people trying desperately to get aboard a plane. "I saw people jamming the door and women and children could not get on," she said. "The shelling came closer and then the plane took off with people still hanging at the door."

Others left by boat. "There was a lot of bombing during the night and the next morning people were rushing to the barges," said Linh Do. "My mother was carrying my two-year-old sister wrapped in a blanket. She had lost her shoes and was running barefoot."

A young Vietnamese girl recalled how she and her family scrambled to board a small boat with 50 other people. "I could hear the noisy firing guns, screams from injured people on the beach, and cries of little children," she wrote later. "While standing on the boat, I couldn't think of anything. It was not until sunset, when it was dark, that I stopped staring back and started worrying about the waves. It rained all night. I was all wet and cold. Holding each other, my brother and I prayed. The next day at noon time, we reached an American ship. As soon as the ship lowered one of its stairs, everybody climbed up the stairs without any order. Men, women, and children were pushed aside and dropped into the sea. Some were crushed between boats. I carried my youngest brother and went up that stairs with fear." During the next

Desperate to leave South Vietnam before the communist takeover, people crowd around a U.S. embassy bus in Saigon in April 1975, waving their citizenship papers. At the time, an airlift was evacuating more than 1,000 people from South Vietnam each hour.

few weeks, 40,000 to 60,000 Vietnamese escaped in boats to the open sea. They were picked up by American navy ships.

The refugees had no time to prepare for departure. Later, more than half reported that they had had less than 10 hours to get ready to leave their homelands. They were driven by fear. "I was afraid of the killings when the Communists came to town," one refugee explained.

Some did not even know for certain who would be going and who would be staying. Said one refugee, "Mother came along to the airport. Then at the last minute she stayed behind because the number of children staying was larger than those leaving." Others thought they would be gone for only a month or two: "My mother would never have left her other six children behind if she thought she wasn't coming back."

Many did not even know they were leaving, or where they were going. "I saw everyone running to the harbor, so I decided to go along," recalled a Vietnamese. One refugee family reached the Philippines only to discover that they were being sent on to the United States. "We did not plan on taking this trip," they later said.

My-lien Dinh was coming home from school on the afternoon of April 28, 1975—a day, Dinh later recalled, that seemed "just like every other day." Suddenly, the street where the Dinh family lived was raked with machine-gun fire from two jets. The children ran into the house and scurried under the bed. "I thought that if a bomb were to hit our house, the bed wouldn't help much," Dinh said later. "Anyway, I guess that seemed the only logical place to hide in such a sudden, stressful moment." Crouched under the bed, listening in fear to the roar of the jets and the rattle of bullets, she realized that the war that had been tearing at Vietnam for years was finally over. The North Vietnamese had won. "The atmosphere in the house was very tense," she said. "Nobody was talking to anyone else. People just stared off into space, lost in their own thoughts."

The next day, an argument broke out in Dinh's family over whether they should remain in Vietnam or go to the U.S. embassy and try to get evacuated to the United States. Her grandmother, the oldest member of the family, had always taken the lead in making decisions, according to Vietnamese tradition and the Dinh family's custom. Now the grandmother did not want to leave her homeland and her husband's grave, and she said unhappily, "I am too old to start life over in a foreign land." Yet Dinh's father insisted that the family should leave, declaring, "I cannot let my children grow up under Communist rule!" Dinh later said, "I could tell that it hurt my father tremendously to make this decision because, for the sake of the children, he was forced to break away from the family unit. Traditionally, Vietnamese families make such decisions as a whole; I can only imagine the suffering my father underwent."

Dinh saw her father crying as they went to the U.S. embassy. She cried too. The embassy was a scene of great disorder, with people scrambling about in confusion. "There were abandoned possessions left by people in a hurry to get away," Dinh said. "Among those possessions were children who had been lost in the shuffle." Hundreds of people were trying to climb the embassy walls, and whenever the door opened, people were trampled in the rush to get inside. The Dinh family waited for hours to get onto a helicopter, afraid that they might not make their escape after all. The sound of enemy gunfire grew louder. Finally the Dinhs ran across the

A group of "boat people," refugees from Vietnam, aboard the freighter Tung An *in Manila Bay in the Philippines in 1979.*

landing field to clamber aboard one of the last helicopters out of Saigon. "As it began to take off," Dinh said later, "all of us held each other tightly because all we had left was each other."

Some 130,000 Vietnamese refugees found sanctuary in the United States in 1975. They generally came from the educated classes. Many of the heads of these households had completed high school and attended college. Almost two-thirds of them could speak some English. Most came from the urban areas, especially from Saigon; they were more Westernized than the general population of Vietnam. After arriving in the United States, the 1975 refugees were placed in processing camps, usually on military bases such as Pendleton in California and Fort Chaffee in Arkansas. From the camps they were spread throughout the country as church groups and American families offered to act as their sponsors, helping them get settled. Often the refugees were the only Southeast Asians, or perhaps the only Asians, in the towns that were their new homes. Soon, however, Vietnamese began to form their own communities in places such as Orange County, California.

At the same time, another group of Southeast Asian refugees was in flight; many would seek sanctuary in the United States. They were from Lan Xang, "Kingdom of the Million Elephants," as Laos was called in the 14th century. An inland country wedged between Thailand and Vietnam, Laos was colonized by the French in 1893. After World War II, Laotian nationalists led by a Communist group called the Pathet Lao began their struggle to overthrow French coloni- alism. Laos was established as an independent state in 1954, and civil strife broke out between the Pathet Lao and the anticommunist Royal Lao for control of the country.

The conflict in Laos merged with the Vietnam War. The Ho Chi Minh Trail, which North Vietnam used as a supply line to the south, ran through Laos. North Vietnam supported the Pathet Lao in order to protect the trail, while the United States gave assistance to the Royal Lao to interrupt the movement of the Communists' troops and military sup- plies. By the 1960s, the Vietnam War had been extended into Laos. The United States increased its operations in Laos through the Agency for International Development (AID) and the Central Intelligence Agency (CIA).

The Pathet Lao gained control of Laos in 1975 and began a campaign of bloody repression. Suddenly the Laotians who had supported the United States scrambled in panic for safety. In massive numbers, they fled to Thailand, where they were forced to live in squalid and crowded refugee camps. By the early 1980s, some 140,000 of them had been resettled in the United States. They belonged to three different ethnic

35

groups: 70,000 of them were Lao, 60,000 were Hmong, and 10,000 were Mien.

The Lao are ethnically and culturally related to the people of Thailand. They are concentrated in the lowlands of Laos, along the Mekong River, and they dominate the country's economy and politics. The Lao regard themselves as a people entirely apart from the Mien and Hmong, who are culturally and even physically different from them. The Mien and Hmong are highland peoples who live in the remote, deeply forested mountain regions of Laos. Both the Mien and the Hmong were targeted for destruction by the Pathet Lao because they had helped the CIA carry out American military operations in Laos. "From 1961 on," said a Hmong man named Houa Thao Vang, now a resident of Fresno, California, "we worked for the CIA." Dang Moua, now a pig farmer in Livingstone, California, revealed, "We Hmong fought what Americans call the secret war in Laos. It was no secret to us." The war inflicted heavy casualties on the Hmong. "We had to move from camp to camp," said Touly Xiong. "Our villages were bombed."

The situation became extremely dangerous after the war ended in 1975. "The Pathet Lao wanted revenge, the extermination of the Hmong," explained Touly Xiong. "I left Laos on June 18, 1975. I had to go or else I would be killed." Xiong escaped alone; others went in groups. "I remember the first evening that people in my village, Ban Nam Hia, Sayaboury, Laos, fled to Thailand," said Ghen Vang. "Before making a decision to flee that evening in June, 1975, the entire village, young and old, men and women, over 1,000 people were outside. . . . They talked and discussed what to do. The goal was decided: Thailand and then America, but it was a dark and unseen goal. The decision was passed along from person to person. At 10:30 P.M. most of the villagers were gone. By midnight all had fled." The refugees trekked to the Mekong River, crossing it on bamboo rafts and inner tubes to Thailand.

Like the Vietnamese, the Lao made their journey hurriedly, in fear and silence. One Lao refugee fled with her family in 1975, when she was less than six years old. Because her parents were carrying the younger children, she had to walk for 15 miles at night through the jungle to the Mekong River. Her parents paid a boatman a large fee—including much valuable jewelry—to carry them across the Mekong in his canoe, which barely held them all. During the crossing the canoe was shot at, but the family arrived safely in Thailand.

A Hmong refugee named Xang Hang was also about six years old when the Communists took control of the region around his village of Phamlav, which consisted of about 10 households. The people of Phamlav decided to leave Laos rather than live under Communist rule. Such a decision did not come easily to folks who had lived their whole lives in a small, peaceful village. "At that time," recalled Xang Hang later, "my world was small. I thought Laos and Thailand were the only two countries in the world, and that the world would end at the point where the sky touched the ground at the horizon."

The men of the village began preparing for the journey, hiding household goods and tools deep in the jungle so that they could not be used by the Communists. The villagers killed their livestock, cooked the meat, and packed cooking pots full of a meat-and-rice mixture. They carried the pots, along with blankets, on their backs.

"The villagers carried their luggage and walked out of their homes with great sorrow," said Xang Hang. "As we walked away from our house, I felt so depressed that even though I didn't cry, tears started streaming down my face. As we disappeared at the turn of a mountain, we crossed the farms where the villagers had labored so hard for many years. At that moment, we all felt like our hearts were sliced crosswise with a sword."

As the villagers of Phamlav made their way through the jungle toward the Mekong River, Xang Hang's family was always the last in the group. His parents had to carry the smallest children, and in addition his mother was expecting another child and could not walk quickly. Finally they reached the river, where boatmen took all of their money for carrying them across. Once across the river, the villagers still had to

The "boat people" crossed dangerous waters in worn-out fishing vessels toward an uncertain future. More than 5,000 of them entered Hong Kong harbor in less than a week in 1979.

walk for many days through the rain to reach the border and the safety of the refugee camps in Thailand.

Refugees from other villages joined them. "Children cried from hunger," Xang Hang said, "and many people became sick. Elders who could not walk died along the way. We saw graves that were freshly covered with dirt and leaves." When Xang Hang's family arrived at the border between Laos and Thailand, they paused, with one foot in their homeland and the other foot outside it. "In our minds," said Xang Hang, "we said goodbye to our lands, farms, homes, and every living thing that we had seen and touched. From there, we would never look back again. It was like a baby being separated from its mother's umbilical cord." Eventually, Xang Hang's family arrived, "poor and hungry," at the refugee camp. They were penniless—"Everything we had was lost: land, home, farms, animals, and tools."

On the day that Thiphavanh Rajphangthong's family left their home in Vientiane, the capital of Laos, the young Lao girl "did not know what the departure was all about." Near the end of their journey was a 15-mile walk to the Mekong; they wore ragged old clothes so that anyone who saw them would think that they were humble peasants returning to their farm. "My parents said that if any of us got caught, the Communists would shoot us without any sympathy," said Rajphangthong. "I grew more than afraid. I grew weaker and weaker. . . . At certain moments I wanted to yell and scream so the Communist soldiers could hear the sound and come follow my family and shoot them, including myself. I would rather see my family and me dead than have us fearing, feeling exhaustion and fatigue. But in another moment, I felt I could bear with the rest of my family and I continued on."

Houa Yang, a Hmong, fled Laos with his family and many fellow Hmong in May 1975. His brother carried the family's spare clothing, his sister carried their cookware, his father carried all their food, and his mother carried her six-month-old child. "I had to walk or they would leave me behind," Houa Yang said. At one point the Yang family was part of a crowd of several hundred Hmong who tried to cross a bridge that was guarded by the Pathet Lao. The Communist troops opened fire on the Hmong. "I could see people crying, being killed, blood and flesh flying everywhere," Houa Yang recalled later. "The majority of these victims were women and children." The Yangs finally made their escape, first to Thailand and eventually to the United States.

A Hmong girl named Yer Chang was five years old when the Communists took over in Laos. "They [the Communists] killed almost all of the businessmen, doctors, and lawyers, and they sometimes killed or raped the women and children," she said. Yer Chang's father, a member of the Laotian army, decided that his family's best chance of escaping death at the hands of the Pathet Lao was to flee to Thailand. Their journey took five years, during which they lived quietly and secretly in the jungle, using leaves for blankets, eating wild bamboo shoots and green bananas, and hunting for meat—fish, crabs, deer, and monkeys. Every month or so the family moved on to a new jungle hiding place, always a little closer to the border of Thailand.

Finally, Yer Chang's family was camped near the banks of the Mekong River, along with hundreds of other refugees. "My parents were afraid we might be captured because many people who had come before us had been caught and sent back to Communist camps," she recalled. "Others

also died of hunger due to food scarcity, and some died of poisoning or air deprivation, especially babies because mothers would cover the babies' mouths too tightly for fear their cries might be heard by Communists."

The refugees built rafts of bamboo to make the crossing. "The floats were paddled back and forth to get about a thousand people across the river that night," said Yer Chang. "By morning, some of my cousins and other Hmongs couldn't make it across because the Communists saw them and shot them down. Jumping from the floats into the rushing water trying to avoid being shot, some of my relatives drowned because they couldn't swim." Yer Chang and her family were among the lucky ones: they reached Thailand and arrived in the United States in 1981.

Many refugees from Laos had to spend as long as five or six years in the terrible camps along the Thai border. Despite relief efforts from church groups and aid agencies

Soldiers lead Cambodian refugees to Thai army trucks for transport to a camp near the Thai-Cambodian border. Life in the camps was grim, and for many refugees the stay stretched into years.

around the world, the camps were unsanitary, crowded, and plagued by robbers and smugglers who preyed upon the helpless refugees. Waiting to hear when they would be allowed to leave and where they would be sent, the refugees were gnawed by worry and insecurity. They tried to rebuild the social order of the villages or towns they had left behind, with community officials, healers, and traders fulfilling their traditional roles, but the social and economic life of the camps was chaotic and distorted. Although they were glad to have escaped death at the hands of the Pathet Lao, the refugees could only regard their long stay in the camps as a time of misery.

Meanwhile, in Vietnam, the fighting had stopped and "everything had fallen into absolute silence, a silence that was so unusual," as one refugee later recalled. Then the new Communist government began reorganizing the society. The government took control of businesses, and private property was seized by the state. People who had been associated with the old government were sent to camps to be "re-educated" in Communist philosophy. Large numbers of city dwellers were forcibly moved into the countryside. Thousands of Vietnamese, particularly urban business and professional people, were ordered to "go to the country to do labour, the hard jobs, to make the irrigation canals, sometimes for one month, sometimes for two, or three months."

A businessman who belonged to Vietnam's ethnic Chinese population later described the mass movement of people who were following the orders of the new rulers: "I remember the choked mute lines of families trudging out of the cities to begin agricultural work in the countryside. They had no prior knowledge of how to do that job, yet they had no choice." Another displaced worker said, "Life was very hard for everybody. All had changed! . . . I could see no future for me in Vietnam, no better life! I wanted to escape."

Thousands did escape—21,000 in 1977, 106,500 in 1978, more than 150,000 in 1979, and thousands more later. They were the second wave of Vietnamese refugees, sometimes called "the boat people." Fleeing the repressive new regime, they took their wives and children aboard crowded, leaky boats, risking their lives at sea. Storms threatened to drown them. Pirates waited to rob them and rape the women. Two-thirds of the refugee boats were attacked by pirates; many boats were attacked more than once.

> *Can you imagine human hair*
> *Flowing all over the sea,*
> *Children's bodies ready to dissolve*
> *As human meat dinners of fish?*
> *But they keep on leaving*
> *As humanity turn their heads away*
> *And still they serenely*
> *Throw themselves into death.*

Thirteen-year-old Thai Dang remembered how she left Vietnam in 1981. "I just wanted to embrace my dear friend, Trang, tightly, telling her that I would be leaving Saigon in an hour, that she would always remain my friend," she said. But Dang had to keep her planned escape a secret. "So, I left briefly, as if chased by a ghost, before they could see my eyes getting red. . . . I was yearning to capture each familiar scene, each beloved face of the place I had lived and grown up." But as Dang and other refugees were on their way to the boat, they were "discovered and hunted like beasts" by the Vietnamese forces. "I ran, fell, and ran for my life in the unknown darkness of a strange forest, totally oblivious to my bleeding wounds," she said. Dang's mother placed her on a small boat and waved goodbye, and Dang wondered, "Who was to guarantee that I would survive in the dark sea?" At sea, the refugees were attacked by Thai pirates. Said Dang, "The pirates, wearing almost nothing but frightening tatoos, jumped into our boat with axes and guns to rob and beat us. The air was saturated with the most disheartening cries. . . . We were literally begging on our knees."

Luong Bot Chau told a similar story. She and her husband, along with several dozen refugees, sailed away on a small vessel. Off the coast of Thailand, their boat was attacked by Thai pirates. The pirates chopped off one of her husband's fingers to get his ring and then tried to slit his throat. "But the knife they had was too blunt," she said later. Instead they clubbed him to death and threw his body into the sea. Then they dragged the young girls up to the deck and systematically raped them. "We heard them scream and scream," Luong Bot Chau cried. "We could not get out, because the pirates had nailed down the hatch."

A woman named Hue described the horrors of a pirate attack on a refugee boat in the Gulf of Thailand. When the pirates approached the boat, Hue and the other women smeared their faces with engine oil and fish sauce, hoping this would make the pirates leave them alone. But the pirates ordered them to bathe and then raped them. Another woman recalled, "The pirates tied [the Vietnamese men] up and threw them into the water. The remaining people were tied up too, and locked in the hold after being stripped of their belongings. After this, the pirates came . . . to pillage and rape people. One person was killed after being dealt a blow with an iron bar.

Another had his finger cut off because he was unable to pull off his wedding ring. . . . Some [of the Vietnamese men] fell into the water and drowned with their hands bound behind their backs."

The flight of the "boat people" presented countries throughout Asia with a problem. Not every country welcomed the desperate refugees or allowed them to stay. Some nations, such as Singapore, discouraged refugees from coming and allowed only a few boats to land. Other countries turned the refugees away, sometimes by force. Many refugees told of landing on the shores of Malaysia, only to be driven back out to sea by armed soldiers.

Phu Gip and his family left Vietnam in 1979, in a boat that was crowded with 782 refugees, packed so closely together that they did not have room to lie down. They were bound for Hong Kong, but a storm forced them to change course and head for Malaysia instead. On their eighth day at sea, they arrived on the coast of Malaysia, but a crowd of Malaysians armed with knives and guns prevented them from landing. They were forced to put out to sea again in a violent storm but arrived safely at a refugee camp in Indonesia a few days later.

Most of the refugees who survived the storms and the pirates eventually landed in Thailand, where they had to live in horrible refugee camps for months, often for years, while they waited to find sponsors who could arrange passage to countries such as Australia, Canada, and France. The majority of them came to the United States.

This second wave of refugees was more diverse than the 1975 group. It included not only educated professionals but also fishermen, farmers, and storekeepers from the coun-

After fleeing Vietnam by boat and being processed in a camp in Malaysia, these refugees found sponsors and immigrated to Iowa. They had escaped political persecution, but in America they faced a new set of challenges.

tryside and small villages. Unlike the earlier refugees from Saigon, most of the second-wave refugees did not speak English. About 40% of them were ethnic Chinese Vietnamese. When China invaded Vietnam in 1979, the ethnic Chinese in Vietnam found themselves caught in the crossfire, and many fled to escape discrimination.

The flood of refugees from Southeast Asia included a third major group, the Cambodians. Like the refugees from Laos, thousands of Cambodians were uprooted and chased from their homeland by war. Their stories are tragic; they were fleeing from one of the cruelest and most violent tyrants that history has ever seen.

Cambodia is located south of Laos, sandwiched between Thailand and southern Vietnam. Like Laos, Cambodia was dragged into the Vietnam War. In 1965, the Cambodian government under the leadership of Norodom Sihanouk began to permit North Vietnamese troops to move supplies through Cambodia. Five years later, Sihanouk was thrown out of power by General Lon Nol of the Cambodian army. Around the same time, the United States extended the war into Cambodia by sending bombers to destroy North Vietnamese supply lines and camps inside Cambodia.

In April 1975, while Saigon was falling to the North Vietnamese, a Communist movement called the Khmer Rouge came to power in Cambodia and temporarily renamed the country Kampuchea. Under its leader, who was called Pol Pot, the Khmer Rouge launched a brutal program to move Cambodia's urban population to the countryside and to destroy all Cambodians who were suspected of having American sympathies. Almost all teachers and doctors were killed. Anyone who spoke a foreign language or wore eyeglasses was suspected of being a Westernized intellectual and was a target for the Khmer Rouge. People who could read, write, or understand French or English soon learned to hide their knowledge if they wanted to survive. One young boy was put in jail for five months simply because his older brother had been a university student.

The years during which Pol Pot ruled Cambodia, or Kampuchea, are remembered by Cambodians as *peal chur chat,* which means "the sour and bitter time." Pol Pot's goal was to rebuild Cambodian society from the foundations up. He started by tearing down much of what was already there.

"Pol Pot killed all the educated and professional people—doctors, lawyers, teachers," said Vacchira Loth, a refugee who escaped to Rochester, Minnesota. "If they knew I had been a medical school student, I would have been killed right away." Under Khmer Rouge rule, some 2 million people, about a third of Cambodia's population, died. Some were executed in mass graves called "killing fields"; others perished from starvation and disease. Fifteen-year-old Channa Cheng described the killing fields of her homeland in a poem for her ninth-grade class in Seattle:

> *The people are hungry. The sun is shining.*
> *The women are working in the rice field.*
> *The babies are crying for their mother's milk.*
> *The guards are standing with arms around guns.*

47

Religion was one of the first casualties of the Khmer Rouge regime. Cambodia had traditionally been a Buddhist land, but under the Khmer Rouge government, monks and nuns were forced to leave their holy places to toil in the fields, and the people were forbidden to worship. Statues and temples were torn apart or pocked with bullet holes.

Pol Pot's government also tore apart the fabric of family life. Husbands and wives were separated, sometimes forbidden to see one another; the women and men were sent to different work camps. The Khmer Rouge ordered that the children of each community must live, eat, sleep, and work in large groups with other children, apart from their parents.

A refugee named Thany Por recalled life under the Khmer Rouge: "My family did not live together because the Khmer Rouge had to have my family separated. My sister and my brother had to be separated from my parents because they were teenagers. . . . My sister missed my family very much. She had to steal a time to come visit my family because when she asked for permission the Khmer Rouge would not give it. . . . They never let people go visit their family, but some people tried to see their family in secret. If the group leader found out, they got killed because the group leader was very strict and didn't let the people run home. It was very difficult to take a chance to run home." A number of Thany Por's relatives were killed by Khmer Rouge soldiers.

"The Khmer Rouge just killed and killed," said Samnang Chea, another refugee. "They didn't care if the people were good or bad. They just killed them." Refugee Sam Tap described the Khmer Rouge practice of brainwashing young children to turn them against their parents: "The Khmer Rouge say, 'You have to kill your teacher, your mother and your father.' These Khmer Rouge tell them bad things. And all of these boys and girls believe them and then they kill their mother, father, and teacher."

Under the Khmer Rouge, life in Cambodia grew steadily more oppressive. The state mismanaged agricultural lands, and crops failed, leading to food shortages and starvation. The Khmer Rouge became ever more violent and unpredictable. For the most part, the people of Cambodia were cut off from the outside world. Pol Pot had drawn a curtain of silence around the country. The borders were closely guarded so that no one could enter Cambodia.

Frantic to escape from the nightmarish Khmer Rouge regime, thousands of Cambodians tried to flee across their country's border into Thailand, but many were killed in the attempt. Two who did manage to escape were photographer Dith Pran and doctor Haing Ngor, both of whom endured horrifying ordeals at the hands of the Khmer Rouge. Ngor told his story in the book *Cambodian Odyssey* (1987); he also acted the part of Dith Pran in the movie *The Killing Fields,* which tells the story of Dith Pran's escape from Cambodia. One refugee later wrote, "In the four years gone by I have lived in Pol Pot's regime. My uncle, my aunt, and my two brothers were killed and buried in the same hole because Pol Pot's elements knew that my relatives were soldiers. Pol Pot's men killed my older sister's husband because they accused him as a political man who betrayed their Communist Party. I live with wretchedness."

During the late 1970s, Cambodia and Vietnam were at war. In 1979, Vietnamese troops invaded Cambodia and overthrew Pol Pot, throwing the country into disorder. Hundreds of thousands of Cambodians seized the chance to make the dangerous journey to freedom. Lona Tiv was nine years old when his father decided in early 1979 to try to take his two children to Thailand. They were all that remained of the family; Lona Tiv's mother and 57 other relatives had been killed by the Khmer Rouge. Lona Tiv's father went to the border and then sent a message telling Lona and his younger sister to join him. They traveled in secret, pretending they were only going to another town. "I didn't want anybody else to know where I was going," said Tiv. "If I told them the truth, I could be forced to stay, or I could have ended up in jail or been killed." Lona Tiv and his sister had to walk for more than a hundred miles to reach the border. "Our last kilometer to the border was a perilous trip . . . a war and danger zone for refugees," he said.

The zone was littered with land mines. "Along the road, there were people dying and suffering from land mines and rocket wounds. . . . The sounds of injured people and children crying for help were everywhere in the woods." The column of fleeing refugees was bombarded with rocket shells; one exploded just in front of Tiv and his sister, killing both parents of a little girl. Another woman died when she stepped on a land mine. After crossing the border, the children had to run a gauntlet of Thai bandits, who robbed the refugees of any valuables they were carrying. They passed the bodies of refugees who had been killed by the bandits. Finally, they reached the safety of the camp and were reunited with their father. A year later, they came to the United States.

By the early 1980s, refugee camps in Thailand were swollen by the tide of people fleeing Cambodia. Life in the camps was difficult; countries around the world were providing food, medicine, and other aid, but there was never enough to go around. The camps were crowded and infested with disease. The refugees also had to cope with the bands of smugglers and robbers who were active in the camps. Rapes and beatings were common. Most refugee families had to endure these conditions for at least a few months before the paperwork that would allow them to set off for a new home was completed. Many waited for years. Eventually, more than 100,000 of them were resettled in the United States.

Some of the Cambodian refugees were educated people from the cities, but most were country folk, farmers from the rural areas. Many were women who had lost their husbands in the Cambodian conflict and had come to America with their children. All of them carry the horrible psychological scars of the war and mass exterminations. "The tragedy during the war hurts inside when I remember what happened in the past," a tenth-grade boy told an interviewer. "I try not to think about it, but at night I dream and see my brother who they killed. I dream about him trying to find us. I dream they keep shooting him and shooting him until I wake up."

Many people in the United States have a hard time even imagining the kinds of experiences that the Southeast Asians passed through on their way to America. An American teacher was using the well-known spelling game called "Hangman" to teach English vocabulary to some refugee students. During the game, the players gradually drew the figure of a person hanging from a tree. Suddenly, one of the Southeast Asian students remarked, "That is how my parents were killed." At that moment, the teacher was reminded of just how much these refugee students had suffered and lost.

Like earlier immigrants from China and Japan, some of the Southeast Asian newcomers found work in the agricultural industry on the West Coast. These women and three others in their family picked asparagus on a farm owned by their sponsors in Washington.

Chapter Three

The Vietnamese in America

REFERRING TO THE VIETNAMESE WHO HAD BEEN forced to flee to the United States, an American veteran of the Vietnam War said, "Remember these are the people who were on our side. They have a right to come to this country as refugees. They just need a home." But often they have felt unwelcome in America. Like earlier Asian immigrants, the Vietnamese have experienced the stings of racial insults. They have been told to "go back to China."

The newcomers from Vietnam have been viewed with dismay by some Americans, especially in areas where there are shortages of housing and jobs. "The presence of the Vietnamese refugees," explained Chuong Hoang Chung, a professor at San Francisco State University, "is viewed as a threat, such as being cheap labor when there is a scarcity of jobs." On the Gulf coast of Texas, Vietnamese fishermen have been the targets of demonstrations and threats by the racist Ku Klux Klan organization. Competition between Vietnamese and white fishermen has erupted into ugly confrontations and violence. "There's too many of them," a white fisherman said, "and there's not enough room for them and there's going to be lots of hard feelings if they don't get some of them out of here and teach the ones that they leave how to act and how to get along." This Texas fisherman went on to offer his own suggestion for how the new arrivals should be treated: "I think they ought to be put on a reservation somewhere . . . or in a compound to teach them our laws and our ways, the way we live, our courtesy as a people."

But the Vietnamese see the situation differently. They simply ask for the same acceptance that has been granted to immigrants from European nations. "It's really hard for you [Americans] to understand us," one refugee said, "and we don't expect you to, but we do expect you to treat us as human beings and not be prejudiced." Conflicts like the one on the Gulf coast have also occurred around San Francisco, where local fishermen resent the arrival of Vietnamese competitors; in eastern Oregon, where Vietnamese people gathering wild mushrooms in national forests to sell to restaurants are viewed as intruders by local whites who have controlled the mushroom trade for years; and in Ontario, Canada, where the Vietnamese are competing to gather worms for sale to bait shops and fishermen.

Many Vietnamese, especially those who fought in the army, have remained fiercely determined not to let their loyalty to their homeland slip away. Their strong anti-communism has made them believe that all Vietnamese refugees should think and feel the way they do. To some extent, this has meant that people within the Vietnamese community whose ideas differ from those of the community leaders have not been encouraged to express themselves freely. One refugee sadly commented in a California newspaper in 1988, "It is ironic that despite their struggle to escape what they considered tyranny in Vietnam, many refugees find that they face another tyranny in this country in the form of insistence on political conformity."

Many Vietnamese patriots, particularly those who arrived in the United States during the first wave of immigration in 1975, refused to acknowledge the end of the Vietnam War. Even after the United States had given up the war, these refugee leaders lobbied Congress to give aid to the "freedom fighters" in Vietnam who were still working to overthrow the Communist government. They formed organizations like the National United Front for the Liberation of Vietnam; their official anthem declares, "Citizens, arise and respond to the call of the ancestorland. . . . Even at the cost of lying dead in heaps, we shall shed our blood to revenge our people." They gathered on Vietnamese holidays and pledged "We shall return!" Yet the Communists have remained in control of Vietnam, even after the Vietnamese army withdrew from neighboring Cambodia, and even after the Soviet Union, the Communist superpower that was Vietnam's major supporter, collapsed in 1992.

During their early years in the United States, many of the Vietnamese refugees saw their exile from their homeland as temporary. They hoped to return to Vietnam someday. A 1977 survey showed that 41% planned to return to Vietnam to live. Their attachment to Vietnam remained strong. "Vietnam is my home," one woman wrote in 1988, after 10 years in the United States. "I get angry, mad, when I see Vietnamese children who can't speak Vietnamese." This included her own children, who were born in the United States. When asked what would happen to her children if she were able to return to Vietnam, she answered, "They will have to choose between the two countries."

The refugees tried to reproduce their traditional culture in the new Vietnamese American communities. But many of them have realized that the old ways could not be strictly maintained in the United States. This was especially true when it came to men's and women's roles. "In Vietnam, the women usually were dependent on the husband a great deal," a Vietnamese man explained. "Then when we came here, the Vietnamese women had jobs. This made the men feel extremely insecure." Some men, he added, were able to adjust to their wives' new roles: "My wife didn't work in Vietnam.

Hindered in his search for a job by his inability to speak English, Mui Tran, once a tea farmer in the highlands of Vietnam, studies the language of his new home at Tacoma Community College, Washington, using a Sears catalog as a textbook.

Now because she is working, I start to help her with the dishes and chores around the house. Sometimes when I am on vacation and she is working, I try new recipes so that when she comes home the meals are ready. She never tells me that I should help her but I think because she is working like me too, I should give her a hand."

Some Vietnamese women have found new opportunities in America. Winnie Che, for example, began working as a waitress in 1981. "My first job I felt so happy," she said. "I can work! Somebody will hire me here." Che saved her money and took loans from family and friends. In 1983, she opened her own restaurant in Carnation, Washington. "In Vietnam, I would be just a housewife: clean up, cook dinner. Here, if you work hard, you can do what you want." Vietnamese women like Winnie Che have begun to stretch themselves away from old roles, freeing themselves for new activities and identities. But these new freedoms have brought conflict to some families. College-educated Vietnamese women who plan professional careers for themselves may have difficulty escaping from their parents' more traditional ideas, which may include marriages arranged for them by the parents.

Thrust abruptly into a very different culture, the Vietnamese have found their traditional family ties severely strained. "Back in Vietnam the family is something precious for us—father, mother, children," explained Tran Xuan Quang. "But in coming here, we saw that the family here is too loose. The father works in one place, the mother works in another and they don't see each other at all. Sometimes the father works in the morning and the mother works in the afternoon and the children go to school. When they get home, they hardly see each other at all."

Sometimes parents are saddened by the new behavior of their children. Living alone in Chinatown in Oakland, California, 61-year-old Pham Hai could not find a job, partly because of her age and partly because she spoke English poorly. She was unhappy about the way her children treated her. "When I was in Vietnam," she said, "I expected my children would take care of me when I got here. But when I got here my children threw me out a short time later. . . . This is very different from my life in Vietnam. Many times I have thought of suicide." Life in the new country is especially hard on older refugees. After 15 years in the United States, many of the older Vietnamese people still mourn the loss of the communities and customs they left behind in the homeland.

Many young Vietnamese Americans have begun to lose their Vietnamese language. "I hated it when Americans teased me about my language," complained Mai Khanh Tran. "Maybe that's why I don't talk in Vietnamese in front of an American anymore. When I first came here, I used to talk in Vietnamese but ever since they teased me I don't feel comfortable doing it anymore. At home I do because my parents always talk Vietnamese and I'm trying to preserve what I have for as long as possible. But I can feel it's slipping away."

Thousands of Vietnamese young people have entered college as high achievers, but others have found themselves on the streets. Many of them had come to America alone, sent by their parents, who hoped that the children would obtain an education and become American citizens. This practice was called "throwing out the anchor." The idea was that once the children became U.S. citizens, they would be able to bring their parents and other relatives to America. Without families, though, many of these Vietnamese children had difficulty surviving. They found themselves living in motels, often sharing a room with three or four other young people, and hanging out in cafes and pool halls.

Some young Southeast Asians have joined gangs; Vietnamese gangs have appeared in Los Angeles, Seattle, and other cities. Most of the gang activities involve petty theft, such as the stealing of stereos from parked cars. But, in 1984, a Vietnamese gang tried to rob a jewelry store in Los Angeles's Chinatown. Alerted by a silent alarm, two police officers arrived on the scene. A shoot-out followed, leaving one officer and two holdup men dead and the second officer wounded. A gang member named Sang Nam Chinh escaped with wounds but was later arrested and charged with attempted robbery and the murder of the police officer.

Chinh's story is typical of the young Vietnamese who have found themselves unable to adjust to life in America. He left Vietnam in 1978, crowded onto a refugee boat with his sister and 350 others. After a year in a refugee camp, he came to the United States. He was placed in the ninth grade in a

California high school, but he was not prepared for American schooling. Life in Vietnam and in the refugee camp had been so disrupted that Chinh had not been in a classroom for six or seven years. He did not know how to read or write Vietnamese, and it was almost impossible for him to learn anything in English. "He really tried the first year," his sister said, "but he would come home and tell me that his classes were too hard. He said he needed help, but none of us knew English." Chinh dropped out of the eleventh grade and then worked for a while as a busboy and a delivery man. Eventually, he became involved with a group of young Chinese Vietnamese called the "black ghost" boys. Vietnamese teenagers like Chinh left their homeland to escape a hopeless future, but in America they have become a "lost generation" of refugees.

An ethnic Chinese couple from Vietnam weds in New York in 1975. The groom, Howard Chan, flew to Saigon just before its fall to rescue the bride; sadly, many family members were left behind in Saigon.

Most Vietnamese have faced adjustment problems in America. Nevertheless, they have begun the process of settling down in their new home. "In their heart they want to go back," Chuong Hoang Chung said. "But reality has crept in and they know they will be here for a long time. They receive letters from home saying conditions are terrible and don't come back. They are also having children born here."

Many Vietnamese want to become part of American society. One refugee pointed out that it was necessary to become American "to some degree" in order to live in harmony with other Americans. "For example," he explained, "if we are strangers in the neighborhood, there might be some resistance from the natives. But if we become their friends and show them that we are nice people too, then their anti-Vietnamese attitude would alter. In fact, if different people understand each other, then there will be a lot less hatred between the races." But many of the new settlers want to be accepted as Vietnamese as well as Americans. "We cannot look at the future without knowing who we are. We must remember our roots, our heritage," insisted one Vietnamese American.

In addition to cultural challenges, the refugees faced economic difficulties. Some were wealthy and arrived in the United States with enough money to open their own businesses, but most needed to find jobs. Yet many of them could not get jobs with the same income and status they enjoyed in Vietnam. Thirty percent of the heads of households among the first wave of refugees had been professionals—doctors, lawyers, teachers, and the like—in Vietnam. Another 15% had been managers. Yet, after two years in the United States, only 7% were working in professional jobs and only 2% were employed as managers. Many Vietnamese turned to jobs in the crafts, such as the building trades, or to service jobs, such as working in stores and hotels.

"In Vietnam I was a history and geography teacher," a refugee said. "Here I worked on many different jobs—brick layer, carpenter, clerk typist, salesman, truck driver, delivery man. I felt frustrated and depressed because I had social status and possessions in Vietnam. Here I didn't have anything." The Vietnamese have also experienced problems of racial discrimination. Some feel that racism has kept them from being hired or promoted. A Vietnamese woman who had worked for a large American bank for several years believed that white men in the bank were promoted faster than she was and received higher salaries than hers. "I'm a U.S. citizen," she said, "but my physical appearance cannot change—I'm still yellow."

"I am a patient man," a Vietnamese refugee said. "If I have to start over again, I believe I will make it someday. I believe I will become self-sufficient as an auto mechanic. Most refugees have only one hope: to have a job and become a tax payer." Many Vietnamese have achieved much more. In California, where 40% of the Vietnamese refugees have concentrated, they have created their own Vietnamese communities. In 1988, the city of Westminster, California, officially named its Vietnamese district "Little Saigon." The neighborhood is a "large language island" within the city. Referring to one of the main streets of Little Saigon, Chuong Hoang Chung said, "A walk down the Bolsa Avenue can testify to the extensive use and importance of Vietnamese. A look at directories published in Vietnamese and distributed free to Vietnamese shoppers shows that any Vietnamese resident of Orange

Nguyen Kim Guyen and her brother, Nguyen Huy Han, opened a successful restaurant in Pontiac, Michigan. Such restaurants sprang up in many cities in the late 1970s, introducing Americans to Southeast Asian cuisine.

County can obtain all necessary services without ever having to use English. From social services to health care and other basic needs, Vietnamese speakers are at home."

Vietnamese own many businesses in Orange and Los Angeles counties. There are a lot of Vietnamese doctors and dentists. Ethnic Chinese Vietnamese operate hundreds of restaurants and grocery stores. Not all of these businesses are small "mom-and-pop" stores. Many of the store owners had been big merchants in Vietnam. They brought substantial sums of money with them to the United States, and now they operate whole chains of stores, such as the Wai Wai Supermarkets and Man Wah Supermarkets.

At first, the Vietnamese-owned businesses served Vietnamese customers. "For people who do business here, they feel as if they are doing business at home [in Vietnam]," said Hoang Giao of the Vietnamese Chamber of Commerce in Los Angeles. Most of the shop signs in Westminster's Little Saigon are in Vietnamese only. But Vietnamese merchants and professionals have begun to reach out for a larger customer market. Some now serve the needs of white, African American, and Hispanic customers and clients.

In northern California, the Vietnamese have begun to flourish as businesspeople, especially in San Jose. "Vietnamese now constitute 10% of San Jose's population and have moved into its commercial life in an aggressive way," reported T. T. Nhu in 1988. "Nearly 40% of the retail business in downtown San Jose is Vietnamese. . . . The fact is that the Vietnamese have become an inescapable presence in San Jose. They want to become part of San Jose because they are here to stay." Downtown San Jose had been in decline, suffering from a loss of business, until the arrival of the newcomers from Southeast Asia. They pulled downtown San Jose up out of its decline. "There's a new vitality downtown and it's the Vietnamese who have made it what it is today," said Doanh Chau, director of San Jose's Vietnamese Chamber of Commerce. "It was abandoned. But the past few years has brought new life to the area."

The signs of Vietnamese American settlement have become a permanent part of the American landscape. Most cities boast Vietnamese restaurants or even whole neighborhoods; many classrooms include Vietnamese students. The refugees who fled in panic in the airlift of 1975 and the boat exodus a few years later have been joined by immigrants arriving in a more orderly fashion. In 1979, the U. S. and Vietnamese governments signed an agreement called the Orderly Departure Program (ODP). Under the ODP, 20,000 Vietnamese have been permitted to leave Vietnam each year to join family members who were already in the United States. They arrive not as refugees in flight but as immigrants.

Another group of immigrants from Vietnam is a legacy of U.S. involvement in the Vietnam War. These immigrants are the Amerasians—children born of Vietnamese mothers and American fathers. They have faced unique problems, both in Vietnam and in the United States. By 1976, there were between 12,000 and 15,000 Amerasian children in Vietnam, the sons and daughters of American servicemen who had fought in the war. The majority of these children never knew their fathers. In addition, their mixed racial heritage made life in Vietnam especially hard for them; often they were rejected and treated as outcasts. As Chuong Hoang Chung explains, "These children grew up in a traditional Asian society that rarely accepts interracial relations." Children who showed the racial features of their white or African American fathers—features such as blue eyes, curly hair, or unusually light or dark skin—were viewed as oddities. They attracted crowds and sometimes suffered from harassment. Chi D. Pham, an Amerasian from Vietnam, described the plight of the Amerasians in a poem called "Crying Drops of Blood:"

> *Who poured these pains over us?*
> *Who can understand orphaned*
> *Children, the foreigners who fathered us,*
> *Diluted our blood and divided us*

In half. Never have we felt
Fully human. Like wandering souls
Without relatives, we have
No temple, no offering.
Ghosts receive respect, we are greeted
With hate. People kick us
Without pity back and forth.

Most of the Amerasian children were desperately eager to come to America. In the early 1980s, a small number of them—generally those whose fathers had asked that they be allowed to come to America—were able to leave Vietnam under the Orderly Departure Program. In 1988, the U.S. Congress passed the Amerasian Homecoming Act, which allowed Amerasians, along with their mothers, stepfathers,

In an East New Orleans neighborhood with a large Southeast Asian population, street signs are posted in English and Vietnamese.

and half-siblings, to enter the United States as immigrants and still receive the aid and benefits given to refugees. The flow of Amerasians and their family members into the United States increased in 1989 and the early 1990s.

The Amerasians traveled to America in several stages. The first stage was to a transit center, built by the United States in Vietnam in 1989. There officials helped the Amerasians get ready to emigrate, guiding them through the long and complicated process of completing the necessary paperwork. Some emigrants lived at the transit center for weeks or even months while their cases were being handled. After leaving Vietnam, the Amerasians usually spent some time in a refugee center in Thailand or the Philippines. From there they were resettled in New York, New Jersey, Pennsylvania, Oklahoma, Alabama, and other states. However, many of the Amerasians and their families have followed the example of other Southeast Asians in the United States by moving to California.

Like other Southeast Asians, the Amerasians have experienced difficulties in adjusting to life in the United States. When Amerasian young people in California were surveyed in the early 1990s, nearly one-third of them spoke of problems with money, housing, or family conflict. Another source of stress was the Amerasians' relationship with the Vietnamese community already present in the United States. When asked how they got along with Vietnamese Americans, the Amerasians spoke of alienation and rejection:

> *They are afraid of us Amerasians.*
> *They don't accept us yet.*
> *They look at me funny.*

They are not sincere.
They look down on you.

A few reunions between American fathers and their Amerasian children have taken place. Many Amerasians would like to trace their fathers, although for most this task is all but impossible. The information they possess about their fathers is often scanty or long out of date. Most are concentrating on building their own futures in America through school and jobs. Half Vietnamese, half American, not fully accepted by either society, they are striving to make a place for themselves and to make peace with their own identities.

Tuan Van Le is an Amerasian born in Saigon. He came to the United States with an aunt at the age of seven, before he had learned to read and write Vietnamese. He went to American schools and grew up with American interests, especially a passion for football; in college, he played on Stanford University's team. Tuan Van Le's childhood in Vietnam was shaped by war, bombings, and battles—things he did not want to remember. For years after coming to the United States, he denied his Vietnamese origins. Finally, in his senior year of high school, a class on the Vietnam War helped him regain his identity. He began learning to read Vietnamese. "Whatever I do, although I do it for myself and my family," he said, "I still try to make Vietnamese proud of me—and through me proud of who they are."

The refugees who fled the Communist takeover in Vietnam feared that they would never be able to go home again. For many years after the war ended in 1975, travel into Vietnam was forbidden to residents of the United States. But by the late 1980s, the Vietnamese government had begun to

Amerasian children in a Vietnamese orphanage in 1982. The children of American servicemen and Vietnamese mothers, the Amerasians have faced unique difficulties in both Vietnam and the United States.

ease its restrictions on travel, allowing Vietnamese who were living in France, Canada, and other countries to visit their homeland. In 1989, 15,000 Vietnamese from abroad went to Vietnam. Few were from the United States, though, because a U.S. ban on trade with Vietnam made it difficult for American citizens and residents to enter Vietnam.

In the early 1990s, the door into Vietnam began to open for Americans. Although Vietnam remained a Communist nation, it was eager to open trade with the United States. A few Americans began visiting Vietnam as tourists, usually entering through Thailand. Then, in 1993, the United States lifted its ban on trade with Vietnam, allowing U.S. citizens and residents to travel freely to Vietnam. That year, about half a million people from abroad visited Vietnam. About 100,000 of them were Vietnamese living in other countries, including the United States.

Although the refugees may visit the land and the relatives they left behind, few of them are likely to return to Vietnam to live. Life in Vietnam seems to be becoming more free and open, but the country is still ruled by the Communist regime from which the refugees fled in the first place. Furthermore, many of them have adjusted to their new life in the United States and have learned to value the freedom and advantages America offers. Many have become U.S. citizens. The younger people, in particular, do not always think of themselves now as exiles from Vietnam. They have become Vietnamese Americans.

A young girl in Laos, photographed in her traditional finery in 1965.
By that time, the United States was recruiting allies among the mountain
tribes of Laos, and that country's involvement in the Vietnam War had begun.

THE REFUGEES FROM LAOS, LIKE THOSE FROM VIETNAM, have found that life in the United States is very different from the life they knew in their Southeast Asian homeland.

"This is a good life here," said a Lao refugee. "No war. No death. No hunger." But many Laotians find American culture almost impossible to understand. "It is easier to move the mountains than get used to American culture," observed a Lao. Another said, "We have been living in a jungle for a long time in Laos. This is another kind of jungle—a technological and bureaucratic jungle."

Kimmakone Siharath knows how hard it has been for his fellow ethnic Lao to make the transition from Laos to America. In Laos, Siharath's family lived in a small farming village outside the capital of Vientiane. His father worked for the government military forces and had to flee when the Pathet Lao came to power in 1975; he escaped to Thailand. A year later, in 1976, Siharath's mother took him and his younger sister across the Mekong River to reunite the family. They remained in Thailand until 1979, when they came to the United States. After living in San Jose, California, for two years, they settled in Arvin, a community near Bakersfield.

"Arvin is like Laos," said Siharath. "It is a small town, a farming community." But Arvin is different from Laos in some important ways. Instead of being surrounded by other Laotians, the Siharath family found themselves a very small minority in Arvin. "I was the only Lao, the only Asian in school," Siharath said. "Most of the students were Mexican, and they called me 'Chino.' They thought I was Chinese." His father worked as a custodian at a high school in Bakersfield, and his mother worked on an assembly line in a factory. "The old people miss their homeland," Siharath said. "In Laos, they owned their land. They were independent and did their own farming. They worked for six months to grow the rice and then stored their crops. They would go hunting and fishing. There was plenty of fresh meat. But here life is stressful. Many Lao are on welfare, and others have low-wage jobs."

The loss of independence was hard to take, Siharath explained. "The old people would like to return to Laos," he said. His father would go back to Laos if the Pathet Lao were no longer in power. "I would like to return too," he added. "No matter how long you are in America, you will always be an Asian, always an outsider, not an American." Siharath has only a vague picture of the square bamboo house where he grew up in Laos. "Inside I wish I could know where my homeland really is," he said. "The little bit of memory from my childhood is burning inside me and I want to be reunited with it."

Siharath applied for U.S. citizenship. "But psychologically I don't feel I'm an American," he said. "I will be what I am only in Laos. America is not a bad place. Still I miss the closeness and friendship of village life in Laos where you could name everybody in the whole village." Siharath's life in America is very different from what it would have been if he had remained in Laos. He enrolled in the University of California at Berkeley to study genetics, explaining, "My parents pushed education. Here education is a necessity for survival. But if I were in Laos, I would not be in college. I would be a farmer now."

A Lao student named Lou Saephan was thrilled with his new life in the United States. "Where I was from, joy was so hard to find," he said. "There had been so many wars going on, people going hungry, and not much hope for the future.

. . . Just enough is grown to keep a family from starvation."
When he and his family left Laos, Saephan took a last look
at his birthplace. "I wanted to be sad," he later recalled, "but
we were moving, hoping to find a better life." After childhood
in a war-torn land and years in a refugee camp in Thailand,
Saephan's first impression of America was positive: "The
neighborhood was so peaceful and quiet. All I heard was
nature singing."

Another young Lao, Syripanomkone Nhouyvanis-
vong, had trouble coming to terms with his Lao heritage after
coming to the United States at the age of 12. "I only wanted
to be an American, I didn't want to be a Lao," he said. "I
didn't care for Laos or the people living there; it became 'over
there,' the far and untouchable place that I had tried so hard
to forget." Nine years later, though, he felt differently: "I am
relearning what Laos was, and I am learning what Laos is
today. I am watching videotapes of Laos, listening to Lao
music, participating in Laotian dance and just doing the 'Lao'
thing. . . . Laos is no longer a far and untouchable country but
a country that bore my being and made me who I am."

The clash between the old and new cultures has been
especially sharp and painful for the Mien and Hmong, most
of whom lived in remote, mountainous parts of Laos, far from
the cities. Life in America has involved dramatic adjustments
for these people. Coming from cultures that did not use
writing, they found it hard to understand how signs and letters
could carry meaning. They were unfamiliar with maps, so that
even when well-meaning social workers provided them with
maps showing them how to get to bus stations and job sites,
they did not know how to follow them. Accustomed to small
communities where everyone knew everyone else, they found

73

Many of the refugees from Laos found it extremely difficult to adjust to life in America. Their knowledge of farming as practiced in their homeland was of little use to them in the United States; some turned to seasonal labor, such as picking berries.

big cities confusing. They felt intensely lost in America, where they had to learn how to use toilets and gas stoves and how to fill out welfare forms. Tasks such as figuring out how to pay a telephone bill became ordeals.

Both the Mien and the Hmong originated in northern China, but although they are similar in many ways, they are two distinct peoples. They speak different languages and cannot communicate with one another. Mien culture has been strongly influenced by Chinese civilization—for example, the Mien eat with chopsticks. In addition, their system of religious beliefs draws heavily upon Taoism, a traditional Chinese faith that recognizes hundreds of deities and countless nature spirits, and upon respect for the spirits of their ancestors, another characteristic of Chinese tradition.

About a million and a half Mien still live in China. The ancestors of the Laotian Mien migrated into northern Laos around 1880 and settled in the mountains. Recruited as U.S. allies in the 1960s, many were evacuated from their home villages in 1967 so that U.S. bombers could bomb nearby Pathet Lao villages. Seven years later, with the victory of the Pathet Lao, thousands of Mien made their way to Thailand. Many eventually came to America; in 1991, there were 12,000 Mien in the United States. Two-thirds of them lived in California.

The story of Vern Ta Seng is typical of Mien experiences in America. Arriving in San Francisco with his wife and six children, he felt helpless, unable to guide his family: "We became handicaps," he said. "We did not know anything. We could not tell if we were alive or not." Vern Ta Seng had trouble renting a house because of his large family; he marveled that in America, a house with five bedrooms might have only four or five people living in it. Finally, he found a dirty house in a bad neighborhood—many of the Mien settled in urban neighborhoods with high poverty and crime rates.

Gradually, Vern Ta Seng and his family learned about life in America. All their knowledge of farming and hunting was useless to them. The children, however, learned English and learned how to study. They went to school and then were able to find jobs when they left school. Vern Ta Seng wanted to keep up the religious rituals that are at the core of Mien life, but he was forced to make some compromises. In Laos, the Mien burned paper "spirit money" as a religious offering; in America, they had to control the fire by burning the money in metal garbage cans. In Laos, wedding ceremonies would be large, festive occasions, involving whole villages and lasting a week or more; in America, said Vern Ta Seng, "We are afraid that it might disturb the neighbors," so weddings last only for two days. "We could not throw away our traditions," explained Vern Ta Seng. "We still have to carry on our religion."

But many Mien worry about whether they will be able to preserve their religion and culture in their new home. In their traditional mountain homeland, the Mien were a nomadic people, often moving from place to place. Because they had no permanent homes, they carried their wealth with them in the form of magnificently ornamented clothing. That practice is being lost. "In America we don't wear our traditional clothing, not even grandmother," said one of them. "We only wear our traditional clothing on special days, and I will make my children only one set of clothes. When they grow up I don't know if they will marry American or Mien, so I will make only one set. Maybe when they grow up, they may forget our language."

The Mien refugees try to keep their traditional culture alive by listening to tapes of sad songs sung by relatives still in camps in Thailand. They tell stories about how Mien villages were destroyed and how they became an uprooted people.

Part of the problem that faces the Mien is that young Mien growing up in America have little or no experience of village life. Many of them, exposed to American values and lifestyles at school, regard their parents as old-fashioned and superstitious. The complex, age-old Mien traditions of community worship and respect for parental authority are breaking down. One Mien refugee sadly predicted, "I am positive the Mien will lose their traditional religion within the next ten years."

The Hmong belong to one of the oldest ethnic groups in Asia. Their name means "human being." In China they are called the Miao. The Hmong came to Laos earlier and in greater numbers than the Mien. The Hmong began entering northern Laos from China around 1820. Today about 2.2 million Hmong—more than 40% of the world's Hmong—live in China. Hundreds of thousands more are scattered

Cheng Chiang Saechao, a Mien, and her children were among the thousand or so Mien who had settled in Washington State by 1980.

throughout Vietnam, Laos, Thailand, and Burma. After the Pathet Lao came to power in 1975, more than 100,000 Hmong fled. These refugees have established Hmong populations in Australia, France, Canada, and the United States. In 1990, there were approximately 90,000 Hmong in the United States. Wisconsin and Minnesota each had more than 16,000 Hmong, and another 47,000 lived in California, especially in and around Fresno in the San Joaquin Valley.

A Hmong proverb says:

> *Cross the river, you'll take off your shoes.*
> *Flee from your country, you'll lose your status.*

Indeed, the Hmong who have left their homes feel a deep sense of loss. In Laos, their lives were intimately bound up with the natural world around them, with the spirits and deities they believe inhabit that world, and with their kin and communities. Away from this familiar environment, they feel that the world is out of joint:

> *In the past, we used to live together in the same village.*
> *Because of the bad years [war], we were forced to leave our*
> *   village to nature.*
> *I, son of the Hmong, came to live in this faraway country,*
> *Not hearing monkeys and gibbons call.*
> *I, son of the Hmong, suffer a life filled with longing,*
> *Having no brothers and relatives to come visit me.*

Tony Vang is one of the few Hmong refugees who had been educated to the high school level in Laos. Yet even though Vang's schooling made him better prepared than most Hmong for the journey to America, he found the transition extremely stressful. He remained haunted by his past. "The first year I spent in America, I made very little progress," he recalled in 1986. "Then I decided: I must forget Laotian. Forget the French I was educated in. Forget Hmong! I must think only in English, only about learning American ways. I struggled along OK in the daytime, but I dreamt every night in Hmong or Lao. It took me three years to dream in English, and those dreams, too, are about the refugee camps, about running away from my country."

Learning English has been hard for the Hmong. Most classes use reading and writing, but the Hmong are not used to the written form of language; the Hmong language was first written down by American and French missionaries in 1953. More than 70% of the refugees never learned to read and write Hmong. English teachers working with the Hmong at a community center in Eau Claire, Wisconsin, have found that the best way to teach English to the Hmong is to teach them first to read and write in Hmong. "We teach them ABCs and apply the alphabet to the Hmong language," said one instructor. "Once they become literate in Hmong, then they can learn English and use the dictionary."

Adjustment has not been easy. "When you pull a plant out of the ground without any soil around its roots—soil from where it was grown—and transplant it, the plant will have trouble surviving," explained Dang Moua, who became a hog farmer in California. "The Hmong never really thought about coming to America, never really believed they would have to leave Asia. Then suddenly we were here. . . . The technology and the Latin language of European or Mexican immigrants are much closer to America's. They have some dirt on their roots."

Many Hmong have been trying to plant their roots in new dirt by farming in Minnesota and California. But their traditional methods of farming do not work well in America. Explained one Hmong farmer, "We don't understand how to irrigate fields. In Laos, farmers just wait for rain. We don't understand marketing—one year farmers get high price for snow peas, next year almost nothing. . . . We thought to ourselves, if we farm, maybe we can be independent people again. But unfortunately, when we arrive in Central Valley [of California] we learn that you must have something else: lots of money."

"We have no other skills but farming—except that we are not farmers anymore," said a Hmong refugee. "We are just unemployed soldiers." But the Hmong feel that the American government has an obligation to them because for many years the Hmong helped the United States in its undercover war against the Communist forces in Southeast Asia. "We fought for 20 years side-by-side with the CIA in the 'secret war.' My brother was killed by North Vietnamese soldiers," recalled Touly Xiong. Almost every Hmong family in the United States lost a father or one or more sons in America's "secret war." The Hmong remember the "promise" the CIA made to them. Said one refugee, "The Americans in Laos had an agreement, a contract with us: 'You help us fight for your country, and if you can't win, we will take you with us and we will help you live.' "

The Americans did bring the Hmong to the United States, but making a living in America has been extremely difficult for the newcomers. "The Americans came to my country and built the war there," one refugee said bitterly. "Now I have no country and I have nothing. When I stayed

in Laos I was a farmer. . . . I had all the things I wanted. I never begged anyone for food. Only when I came to the country of America I had to beg."

Both the Mien and the Hmong have found that Americans generally do not know who they are or why they are in the United States. They have often been mistaken for Chinese and insultingly called "chinks." In Eau Claire, Wisconsin, Hmong names stand out in the telephone directory, and the Hmong receive hostile phone calls. Angry voices tell them, "Go back to your country." Reflecting on the rejection the Hmong have experienced, Chou Lee of the Hmong Community Center in Eau Claire said, "Racism is like a wall. You cannot break through it."

Employment has been a desperate problem for the Mien and Hmong. Some try to make ends meet by selling

Some Mien and Hmong immigrants suffered from extreme isolation, cut off from the familiar life of their villages and unable to participate in the life of American communities in which they had been resettled.

handicrafts like needlework, silver bracelets, and earrings or by doing housecleaning and yard work. Most do not have jobs. In some communities, their rate of unemployment reaches over 60%. After fleeing from Laos in 1975 and spending five years in a refugee camp in Thailand, Choy Spaha reached the United States, where he held a series of jobs in Alabama and California. "I speak Lao, Thai, Mien, English, some Chinese," he said, but he was unemployed and was trying to improve his English by taking classes in Oakland, California. The Hmong may be in danger of becoming a permanent welfare class. A 1987 California study showed that many of the long-term welfare families were Hmong. Sadly, most Hmong are barely surviving.

Some have not survived. Seemingly healthy Hmong men have died suddenly and mysteriously. Doctors unable to explain their deaths refer to the "Hmong sudden-death syndrome." Said one medical examiner in Minnesota, "We're really quite baffled." The doctors have ruled out nerve gas, which was used in Laos, for only men have been affected. By 1988, more than 100 Hmong men had died. Kai Moua of the Hmong Community Center in Eau Claire said, "They're all men, about 30–50 years old. They had been soldiers for 15–20 years. They don't know how to start life over again. They don't know how to farm or to work in a factory." They also felt deep grief, despair, and confusion. Moua described what happened to one of his relatives:

> My cousin almost died one night. He was healthy, but he thought about his parents in Laos and missed them. When he was sleeping he felt pressure like some air

in his lung that went up to his heart and he couldn't breathe and he tried to push the air back down.

Touly Xiong's 48-year-old brother-in-law died from the sudden-death syndrome. "My sister had gone to ESL class [English as a Second Language] that night and when she came home she found her husband depressed," Xiong said. "He said he felt lonely and missed home. They went to bed and around 3 A.M. she woke up. Her husband was making a choking noise and then died."

Some of the Hmong also suffer from what is called "survivor guilt." They are troubled by the twists of fate that spared them but claimed the lives of so many relatives and friends. Vang Xiong, who was stricken by the sudden-death syndrome but survived, said, "Why should I live while others died [in the war]?" Another refugee said, "I shouldn't be alive while better men than me, like my elder brother, are dead."

Depression is widespread among the survivors. "The Hmong were kings of their area in the mountains," explained Tou-Fu Vang, who worked in a U.S. government refugee-resettlement program. "Now they find themselves in a situation that is completely out of their control." A journalist who wrote about the Hmong community in Fresno, California, in 1986 said that many of the Hmong had withdrawn from the world:

> . . . the most striking aspect of the 18,000-strong Hmong community here is its near-invisibility. Concentrated in boxy, airless low-income housing projects . . . they remain indoors much of the time, reportedly for weeks at a stretch. Children are more evident than

Members of the national music and dance company of Laos fled their homeland in the late 1970s and made a new start in the United States.

adults, and mothers more than fathers. . . . The older Hmong, say refugee workers, are simply afraid of the street, but younger Hmong men stay out of sight because they are deeply ashamed of having nothing to do.

Many Hmong in Wisconsin sit by their windows, feeling lonely and sobbing uncontrollably. "My father wakes up with nightmares about three times a week," Touly Xiong said. "He is asleep and then I hear him screaming, 'Get out! Get out! The Communists are coming!' I would like to take him to a counselor. We keep our problems bottled up. Just to tell our stories and have someone listen would help us." A counselor at the Asian American Medical Clinic in Oakland, California, said that the Hmong's depression was making it harder for them to cope with life in America: "If people are depressed, how can they get a job or listen to an ESL teacher?"

Some of the Hmong, along with other refugees from Laos, Vietnam, and Cambodia, have begun to tell their stories. A number of schools, universities, and community centers have gathered the refugees' stories and drawings about their experiences into books for use by teachers and students. In Philadelphia, teenage refugees told their stories in comic book form for an art exhibit that toured the city's schools. The refugees hope that such projects will help others understand who they are and how they came to be in America.

In their struggle to live, to overcome their nightmares, the Hmong express their sorrow in song:

> *Oh heaven, we Hmong did not want to flee from our country*
> > *to a new country*
> *So far that we can no longer see our land*
> *We hear the birds singing, they fly in the sky*
> *They make us feel so lonely*
> *The sun is shining brightly*
> *Are you as lonely as I am, or not?*
> *I still have relatives back in my native country*
> *I miss them more than most people can miss anyone.*
> *My life in this country is sunny; it makes me feel like asking,*
> *"Should I continue to live or is it better to die?"*
> *I have no parents or relatives, only myself alone*
> *Do you know how lonely I am?*

Kao Vang, a Hmong who resettled with his family in California, worried that the traditional closeness of the Hmong community might disappear in America. "The Hmong people still love each other and worry about each other, and they run to help each other," he said. "But in fifteen years they might just forget. The young people don't want to

In an apartment complex inhabited by many Southeast Asians, women exchange goods in the traditional barter system of village economics.

do that; they want to do like this country. If they can speak English good and can support their families they won't worry about the old people. If we had our own country," he added sadly, "we could keep our customs, but if we don't have our country it's very hard."

Younger Hmong are gradually making an adjustment to America. They have learned to speak and write English, and many have pursued higher education. A 1987 study of 10 Hmong communities showed Hmong entering the universities and the professions. In Providence, Rhode Island, with a Hmong population of 2,300, 90% of Hmong who graduated from high school went on to college. In St. Paul, Minnesota, with a Hmong population of 8,000, 130 Hmong graduated from high school in 1986; 80% of them went to college. That same year, 23 Minnesota Hmong received two-year or four-year college degrees.

Many of the younger Hmong do not remember the old country. "Laos is like a dream," said Mao Yang, a college student in Wisconsin who escaped from Laos in 1976 at the age of eight. Her goal is to graduate with a degree in restaurant management and to own a restaurant in California someday. California appeals to young Hmong living in places like

Wisconsin. "There are more Asians there," said Chou Vue, a student at the University of Wisconsin. "People don't look at you. Also I feel much more taller in California." Hmong college student Nou Xiong said that she felt like an "outsider" in Wisconsin and "more blended" in California. These young people see themselves as Hmong Americans and plan to make the United States their permanent home. A young Hmong woman named Nou Xiong was asked if she would go back to Laos if her parents did so. She answered, "No." Then she was asked, "But what if your future husband wanted to go back?" With a smile, she replied, "Oh, he can go."

But the older Hmong and Mien spend much of their time in sadness. "Our village in Laos was ideal," an old Hmong grandfather recalled. "The mountains for rice fields were endless. There were big forests with game to hunt. Good streams. Bamboo. We never had to move far like other villages. Not until the Communists came."

A Mien refugee said, "What I miss the most from Laos is my cow. I raised cows in the mountains. . . . Sometimes they would come from the jungle, and I would ride on the back of one cow." The Hmong and Mien are deeply and spiritually attached to the land they were forced to leave. "In Laos we believed there were spirits in the mountains," a refugee in San Diego explained. "Here, maybe the American Indians believe in spirits, but those"—pointing in the direction of the nearby Laguna range—"are *their* mountains, not ours."

Cambodian refugee Kim Chit Chuom, tutoring a fellow Southeast Asian in English, lost her husband to war and her baby son to starvation before finding sanctuary in the United States. "I want to stay here all my life," she said of her new home.

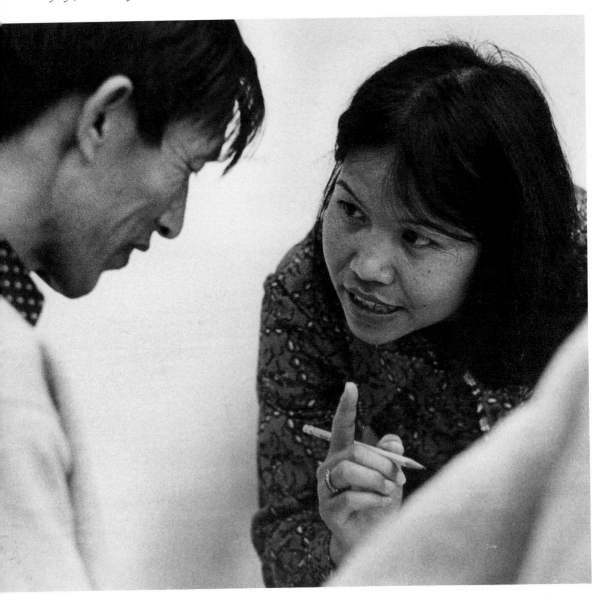

Chapter Five

The Cambodians in America

THE CAMBODIAN REFUGEES HAVE FACED THE SAME challenges as the Vietnamese and the Laotians in adjusting to life in America. One young refugee listed the most confusing things about the United States:

> There is a lot of traffic in this city [Chelsea, Massachusetts]. It's a noisy city. It is confusing to go from one place to another. I get lost all the time. . . .Very often I see women wearing shorts and sleeveless blouses. Cambodian women are much too shy to dress this way. Americans move quickly. Everyone is busy and in a hurry. People often speak in loud voices, even the women. In Cambodia, life is slow and quiet. Maybe that is better. I don't know. . . . American young people sometimes touch older people's heads. In Cambodia we never do that. It would be rude and it's very impolite. . . . Sometimes I don't understand what happens around me. I can't believe what I see. I think this is called culture shock. I can't decide which culture is better. I hope things get less confusing. I know I must try to understand this new country.

In addition to the difficulty of getting used to a new country, the Cambodians also carry the heavy weight of suffering, sometimes for years, under the Khmer Rouge regime before they escaped from Cambodia. Many Cambodian refugees suffer from what psychiatrists call "post-traumatic stress disorder"—a depression that also afflicted the survivors of the World War II Nazi concentration camps.

One who has suffered from severe stress was a 35-year-old Cambodian woman living in Oregon. Although she was safe in America, she found that she could not overcome the horror she had witnessed and experienced. After her husband was executed and her 18-month-old daughter had starved to death, she escaped to Thailand with her remaining children. She had left the killing fields behind, but the killing fields did not leave her. In Oregon each night "she would fall asleep, and in her dreams people came to kill her. During the day she was jumpy and easily startled, and when night came again she told herself to stay on guard and not fall asleep." She became depressed and lost weight. With memories of the extermination still fresh in their minds, still haunting them, many Cambodians have experienced recurring nightmares, emotional numbness, loss of appetite, and withdrawal.

Some Cambodian women have suffered from a strange condition that doctors have not been able to explain: either in Cambodia under the Khmer Rouge regime, or after fleeing from Cambodia, they lost their eyesight. Some became only partially blind, able to see shapes or degrees of light and dark. Others lost their sight entirely. Some have regained their lost vision, but most have not. No one knows for certain how many Cambodian women have been affected this way, but doctors in California alone treated nearly 150 of them between 1982 and 1989. The doctors could find no medical explanation for the blindness. Psychologists have suggested that the blindness is the mind's way of reacting to the horrors the women witnessed in Cambodia—starvation, tortures, beatings, and executions, sometimes of their own family members.

Long Eang is one of the women who have lost their sight. After the Khmer Rouge came to power in 1975, they ordered everyone to leave the town where Long Eang and her family lived. Long Eang, her husband, and their three children joined the line of confused, frightened people marching into the countryside. Long Eang's children were taken away by soldiers to live in a children's work camp. Long Eang and her husband were set to work in the fields. Long Eang's blindness began after some of her relatives were killed by the soldiers; her infant nephew died when a soldier swung his head against a tree trunk. When she saw their bloody clothes, she fainted, and when she awoke, everything was black and she could not see. Later, she recovered partial sight, but her vision was never the same as it had been before the killings.

Long Eang spent four years in the labor camp. She and everyone else suffered dreadfully from hunger. The sight

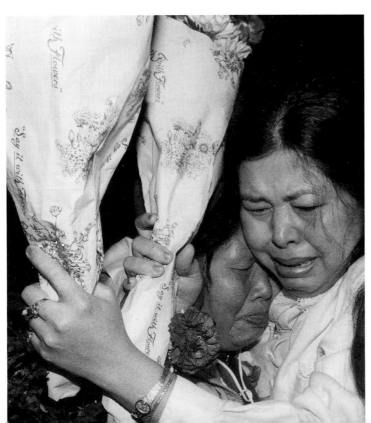

A Cambodian mother and daughter are reunited in a Boston airport after almost a decade of separation, during which the daughter lived in the United States and the mother and 12 other family members remained in a refugee camp in Thailand.

of people dying from starvation became common. Her eyes continued to trouble her, and her sight often faded away into darkness, especially when she worried about what would become of her children. After the Vietnamese invaded Cambodia and overturned the Khmer Rouge government, Long Eang and her family escaped to Thailand, where they spent three years in a refugee camp. An American doctor there tried to treat Long Eang's eyes but could not discover what had affected her vision.

The family came to the United States and eventually settled in California. The horrors of Pol Pot's killing fields are now distant in space and time from Long Eang's new life, but her eyesight has not returned. She may never be free of the burden of suffering she has endured. Her nightmares and memories seem as real to her as the world around her.

Many of the resettled refugees are haunted by their uncertainty about the fate of family members from whom they were separated. After years of trying to locate his loved ones in the refugee camps, one man wrote:

> I did not know if my other sons and daughter or mother had been killed by the Pol Pot regime or tortured by them or starved. It was that way for five years and all the bad stories came out of Cambodia. Then the Vietnamese invaded, and there were more bad stories. I swam in my tears of misery until they were dry, and when I pleaded for help, people would tell me to be patient. I say to the United States, help me or shoot me. Don't tell me to be patient again. I was patient for five years.

Cambodians would like to return to their homeland someday, but they realize the possibility is remote. Well into the 1990s, the Khmer Rouge continues to be a powerful and dangerous force in Cambodia, although it no longer rules the entire country. Many of the refugees who fled the Khmer Rouge have decided to make America their new home. "We want a chance to become part of this country," said one. "It is a chance for a new life. But, inside, the memories are still there. We won't ever forget."

Although the memories of their suffering remain strong, some of the older Cambodians are afraid that their

In a scene from the movie The Killing Fields, *Haing Ngor portrays Dith Pran, who survived the horrors of the Pol Pot regime and eventually made his way to the United States.*

A girl carries water to her family in the Ampil refugee camp in Cambodia. After the nightmare of war, tyranny, and flight, many refugees had to endure months or years of misery in crowded, squalid camps.

children and grandchildren will lose touch with Cambodian culture and customs. "The Cambodian culture is still alive now [in America] because the older people are still alive and are working very hard," said Sam Phay, a community leader in the Tenderloin neighborhood of San Francisco, where many Cambodians have gathered. "But the children don't know about our culture so I worry that our traditions and our culture might die sometime in the future."

Phay is a traditional healer and former Buddhist monk. "People respect him as an old and wise person," wrote

a Cambodian journalist in San Francisco. "He is the only one [here] who has great knowledge about the ways of the Cambodian Buddhist traditions. When there is a problem in the community, people call him—both sides. When people get sick or have some kind of illness, they call him and ask for help." Phay also serves as a matchmaker, advising parents about marriage partners for their sons and daughters, and he gives informal lessons in Cambodian history and Buddhist philosophy.

Phay is one of the hundreds of Southeast Asians— Vietnamese and Laotians as well as Cambodians—who have given new life to the seedy, run-down Tenderloin district. Their shops and restaurants have blossomed in storefronts that were formerly empty or covered with dusty boards. Long blighted by drugs, crime, and homelessness, the Tenderloin is slowly becoming a multicultural neighborhood where Asian, Hispanic, African American, and white families are taking root.

The change in the Tenderloin is partly due to the Cambodian refugees who settled there because rents were low. "Since I came here in 1981," said a Cambodian woman in 1987, "it is cleaner here, more police here, less drug dealing here." Journalist Sophath Pak said, "[The Tenderloin] is like a village, because it is a lot different from two years ago. I can walk at night to visit my friends. It's like back in Cambodia." Half of the Tenderloin's residents are from Southeast Asia, and 70% of the children in the district are Southeast Asian.

Other Cambodians have clustered around Stockton, California, where they work as agricultural laborers; in Chelsea and Amherst, Massachusetts, where many church groups that helped refugees come to the United States are located; and in New York City.

The younger Cambodian refugees focus on the future rather than the past, but they often find themselves trapped between the two. Sathaya Tor, for example, had slaved for four years in a Khmer Rouge child labor camp. In 1979, the 12-year-old boy crossed minefields to escape to Thailand; he came to the United States two years later. In 1988, he enrolled at Stanford University, where he was the only Cambodian student. "Nowadays, sometimes I feel like a frog jumping from one world to the other: school, my family, being American, being [Cambodian]," Sathaya reflected. "In a way to be assimilated in another culture, you have to give up your own culture. With one foot in each culture, the wider you have to spread your legs, the more you could lose your balance. I'm at a point in my life where for the first time I feel vulnerable, and it's scary."

Another Cambodian refugee, Chanthou Sam, can understand Sathaya's feelings. She arrived in the United States in 1975 at the age of 12. Six years later, in recognition of her scholastic achievement and friendly personality, she was elected by her fellow students to be the Rose Festival Princess in Portland, Oregon. She spoke of her ambition to become an accountant, but admitted that this dream was at odds with her traditional culture: "A Cambodian woman is supposed to sit at home, cook, and clean house. I want to be somebody. I want my own job, house, and car before I marry. I want to be independent. It is very hard to be caught in the clash of cultures."

One young man attended a university on the West Coast; there he served as president of the Cambodian students'

association. He was grateful to the many non-Asian students who took part in an effort to raise money to aid the Cambodian refugees, but he recalled a sense of remoteness among Americans, a feeling that he was different from them. His own identity hovered somewhere between Cambodian and American. He remembered looking at himself in the mirror in the mornings and saying, "Good morning":

> It sounds really strange. It seems like there is another person right beside me. I say, hey who are you really? Where does that come from? Why do I speak English? It's very hard for me to feel at ease.

Working by hand in a region where other farmers rely on modern machinery, a group of Cambodian refugees grows beans, broccoli, and melons on their California farm. A tepee serves as both shelter and packing shed.

A group of Cambodian children from the Tenderloin district of San Francisco mug for the camera on their way to school.

Some of the young refugees tried so hard to fit into their new lives in America that they forgot the Cambodian part of themselves. Horng Kouch, who arrived in the United States at the age of 11, tried to put Cambodia behind her:

A couple of years ago, I never thought about my own country after it had become Communist. Everything was broken into little pieces and many hundreds of thousands of people died. I just said to myself, "Forget all about it. It's not worth it. It's the past. Let's just forget all about it." Suddenly I realized that that was not right. I was born there and I should remember it. I was very young then, I knew very little about my culture. Studying at the university I have learned many things about my parents' beliefs and attitudes. I think that some of my classes have helped me in dealing with my Southeast Asian heritage. For some time I didn't even know who I was, whether I was an American or whether I was a Cambodian. Now I know so much about my cultural background that my family is very proud of me.

Other young refugees are also studying the history and language of their native land. They ask their surviving relatives to tell them stories about their families and homes in Cambodia, and they attend traditional festivals and dance performances, learning to appreciate the culture that was almost wiped out by the Khmer Rouge. Although they are firmly planted in American soil, they feel a new affection for their Asian roots. They are creating a dynamic dual identity as Cambodian Americans.

*Five years after fleeing Vietnam on a fishing boat, Tung Dang had
mastered English, graduated from high school and college, and found a job
with a major electronics firm. Through patience and hard work, many of the
Southeast Asian refugees have created bright futures for themselves.*

YOUNG SOUTHEAST ASIAN AMERICANS FEEL MANY stresses and strains. Some of them are still grieving for parents and other family members who were killed in the war or on the trek from the horrors of war. Some belong to families that bear deep psychological scars, especially Cambodian families that endured Pol Pot's regime in the 1970s. Said a San Francisco social worker, "These families spend a lot of time just coping with the past." Such families do not always have the strength or resources to give full support to troubled teenagers.

The teenage years are a time of turmoil and rebellion for most young people. They can be especially difficult for the children of Southeast Asian families. These young people are caught between their parents' customs and values and the lifestyles they see other American teens following. A 15-year-old Cambodian boy argued with his mother over whether or not he could get an earring. She said no. In Cambodia, he would most likely have bowed unquestioningly to her authority. But in Seattle, he defied her and got *two* earrings, causing further trouble at home. An 11-year-old Laotian boy disagreed with his parents about clothes. He liked to wear the clothes favored by other kids his age: baggy pants and a down jacket. His parents, however, wanted him to wear the clothes that they believed were suitable for a young man: dark trousers and a white shirt.

Issues such as dating can create conflict in a household. Because dating as it is practiced in the United States is foreign to Southeast Asian customs, parents usually forbid their children to go on dates or even to spend time with friends away from home. Some parents become somewhat more flexible as they grow accustomed to American ways. In other cases, however, young Southeast Asian Americans reject their parents altogether and run away from home.

In early 1994, social workers and police reported a growing number of Southeast Asian runaways, some as young as 11 or 12 years old. In Seattle, which has a large Southeast Asian population, counselors estimated that as many as one-third of all refugee families had a runaway child. Some of the runaways join the Asian street gangs that have become highly visible in some communities since the 1980s. But most are simply confused, isolated, and unsure of where they belong—like runaways from other ethnic groups.

The great majority of young Southeast Asian Americans, however, are adjusting to life in the United States. Driven by memories of early poverty and suffering, and supported by strong family ties, they are highly motivated to succeed. "If you look at who become National Merit scholars, valedictorians and winners of national music contests," says a professor at Northwestern University, "a lot of them are Southeast Asians."

Phua Xiong is one of many Southeast Asian refugees who has overcome great obstacles to achieve success in the new homeland. To do so, she has had to create her own balance between two worlds: the world of her Hmong heritage and the world of modern America.

Xiong was born in 1969 in the small village of Na Nyong, a collection of huts roofed with banana leaves in the highlands of Laos. Her father was a farmer. He was also a shaman—a wise and holy man who, the villagers believed, could communicate with the spirits. To the Hmong, the natural world is full of spirits. They live in plants, animals, and even rocks. Shamans like Phua Xiong's father performed

rituals to keep the villagers in harmony with the spirit world. Xiong's father was a healer; the villagers came to him for help when they were injured or ill.

Xiong's mother was skilled in *paj ntaub,* the art of Hmong embroidery. In addition to taking care of her nine children, she stitched colorful embroidered decorations onto their shirts, dresses, and pants. But most of her handiwork had to be abandoned when the Communists invaded the region in 1975. Along with thousands of Hmong, Xiong's family fled their home. They went first to Vientiane, along steep, twisting mountain trails and across narrow log bridges. Six-year-old Phua Xiong and the other small children were strapped to horses for the journey. In Vientiane, Phua Xiong's father gave his life's savings to a boatman who agreed to take them across the Mekong River.

The river crossing was hazardous. Soldiers guarded the riverbank. The refugees waited until noon, when most of

A Vietnamese family begins a new life in Illinois in 1975. Strong family ties have helped many refugees survive and prosper, yet Southeast Asian children growing up in America feel the tension of being pulled between two cultures.

the soldiers would take a nap after eating. "It was pretty scary, because nobody could make a sound," Phua Xiong recalled years later. "It's like sneaking out. There are soldiers at every place. At the time, the soldiers are usually fast asleep. That's when you go." The boat that crossed the river ahead of the Xiongs' boat was fired on from the riverbank, and some of the Hmong aboard were wounded. But the Xiongs reached the other side safely and found sanctuary in a Thai refugee camp.

The Xiong family lived in the camp for a year. It was the year in which Phua Xiong was supposed to have begun learning the art of *paj ntaub* embroidery from her mother, but there were no materials and no opportunity for her mother to teach her. "I didn't have a chance to start," Phua Xiong said, "because everything was in chaos." Life was to remain chaotic and confusing for the Xiongs for some time.

Eventually the Xiong family was sponsored by a Lutheran church in Mansfield, Ohio, which arranged for them to come to the United States. During the long plane trip to America, the refugees were served something they had never seen before: a strange round kind of meat. "It was hamburgers," Xiong later realized. "Nobody ate it." Ohio was full of strange new things. The Xiongs had never been inside a Western-style house. Now they found themselves living in one. It had a refrigerator, a bathroom, and water faucets. Their sponsors had to show them how to use everything.

Phua Xiong entered the second grade at a local school. She was the only Asian there, and she felt like an outsider. "Going to school was very painful," she later said. "Every day, I hid behind the doors of the classroom. The other kids played outside. . . . I felt very different, very strange. I didn't see anyone like me."

Xiong's parents, too, were "very lonely and sad," so far from everything and everyone familiar. Xiong's father had been given a job building swimming pools, but he was not successful at the work because he spoke almost no English and knew little about construction. It was hard for him to make the adjustment to his new life. In Laos, he had been a respected village leader, but in America he was a laborer who depended upon help from others.

In the meantime, a number of Hmong had settled in Philadelphia. The Hmong community there included a relative of the Xiongs who invited them to come live in his home. Eager to join other Hmong, the Xiongs moved to Philadelphia. Phua Xiong's father found work cleaning motel rooms; later he got a job in a factory.

The first day of school for a young Vietnamese girl. After learning English in school, such children often become interpreters and guides for their parents and older relatives.

Powelton, the Xiong's West Philadelphia community, was multicultural; Phua Xiong's third-grade class included other Hmong children, as well as Lao, Vietnamese, and Cambodian kids. Sadly, though, racial tension was present in the neighborhood and the school. Xiong and the Southeast Asian children were called "chinks" and tormented by other students. "Children threw things at us," Xiong recalled. "They tried to trip us up. They bothered us when we were jumping rope. They threatened us after school. . . . We sort of had to fight our own battles. It wasn't easy because many of us don't speak up. I didn't speak up because I didn't have the courage to." The wounds of racial insults and harassment still stung years later, when Xiong wrote, "At times when I could no longer control my anger, I let it burst, but only into tears."

Phua Xiong was lucky. She had a sensitive and understanding third-grade teacher who helped her and the other

Southeast Asian refugees at a meeting of the Commission on Human Rights in Massachusetts.

Southeast Asian students improve their English-language skills. He taught her to read and write and encouraged her to keep a diary in English so that she would get used to thinking in English. After a full day at school, Xiong went with her parents to their English classes in adult education. She quickly mastered the language. Like many children in immigrant and refugee families, Xiong became her family's "interpreter," helping family members read their mail and get around in the city. "In the fifth and sixth grade, I used to tutor my aunt, who was going to community college," she said. "I also took people to the hospital and the dentist, and to the welfare office."

As time went on, Xiong became aware of an uncomfortable feeling, as though she was being pulled between two worlds. She began to feel a pressure to fit in to American society, and this sometimes made her ashamed to be Hmong. The conflict between old and new ways could spring up at anytime. It might involve clothing, or the need to choose between her parents' values and her schoolmates' values, or something as simple as her lunch. "I wanted to bring rice to school," she said. "I always felt ashamed to eat it because other students had sandwiches. . . . I couldn't buy the things they bought. Eventually, I stopped eating rice and I ate in the cafeteria."

Xiong did well in school—so well that she was accepted into a high school for gifted students. There she studied hard. "I love books, I love learning," she said. And she had a dream: to go to college. "I was determined I would not be washing dishes and sweeping floors the rest of my life." Many nights she studied until one in the morning, then rose at five to prepare breakfast for her family.

Racial violence troubled Xiong's community in the mid-1980s. Tensions between African Americans and Asian Americans were on the rise. In 1984, a Hmong man was beaten in Xiong's neighborhood, and she remembers that Hmong families lived in fear at that time. Insults were shouted at Hmong on the streets, and bricks crashed through the windows of their homes. "I would get very scared if I saw black guys walking toward me down the street."

But Xiong also made black friends, and after training to be a community organizer she spent six weeks working in a Rhode Island housing project occupied by African Americans and Hispanics. The experience broadened her own sense of racial tolerance and taught her to recognize the things that she had in common with other minorities in the United States.

Xiong was able to fulfill her dream of attending college. She received a science scholarship to Haverford College, located just outside Philadelphia. At first, Xiong's father did not like the idea of his daughter going to college. According to Hmong custom, girls were usually married at 13 or 14, and women were expected to be wives and mothers, not to lead independent lives. But Xiong's mother supported Xiong's decision. "As a young girl," Xiong's mother explained, "she didn't get a chance to develop as she wanted to." She wanted to give her daughter that chance. Xiong's father, too, came to take great pride in his daughter's academic goals.

In the spring of 1991, Phua Xiong graduated from Haverford with a bachelor of science degree. She was the first Hmong in the Philadelphia area to complete college—and one of the first Hmong women in America to do so. At her graduation party, Xiong announced that she had been accepted as a student at the Albert Einstein Medical School in

New York City. She planned to become a doctor. Xiong realized that her ambition made her a subject of considerable interest to the entire Hmong community. "If I succeed, it will be seen as something great and used as a role model," she said. "If I fail, I will be the reason [Hmong] daughters should not go to college."

Going to medical school was not Xiong's only victory. Perhaps equally important, she had begun to make peace with her Hmong identity. Far from being ashamed to eat rice in school, she had learned to value the elements of Hmong tradition, such as the *paj ntaub* fabrics she received as graduation gifts. "I cannot forget that I am Hmong," she said. "A lot of Asian Americans who have gone on to higher education do not come back and serve their community. I don't know if I could change that, but I can make sure I won't be like them."

After completing her medical studies, Xiong said, she would practice among the Hmong in America, using her medical training as well as her knowledge of the Hmong language and culture to improve the lives of her fellow refugees. She had another dream, too—one that might one day help build a bridge between her old and new worlds. She hoped that someday she would be able to go back to the highland village of Na Nyong. "I imagine the houses are torn down or burnt down, or some might be standing," she said, speaking of her childhood home. "I imagine most of the trees have probably been destroyed. I imagine people just struggling to survive." Phua Xiong's dream was to spend some time there as a doctor.

The Southeast Asian Americans are a diverse part of the Asian American population. They have come from different countries, cultures, and classes. They include tribespeople

from the mountains as well as college-educated professionals from the cities, welfare families as well as wealthy businessmen, and high-achieving university students as well as members of youth gangs. But despite their differences, the Southeast Asians share something unique. They came to America as refugees, not immigrants. Their experience has been different than that of the Asians who came to America before them.

Fleeing the horrors of war, they departed in panic, not knowing the country of their destination. They experienced the trauma of refugee camps and the terrible feeling of wondering whether they would have a place to begin life again. They worried about how they would be received when they reached their destination. Would they be welcomed or rejected? More than the earlier groups of Asian immigrants, the Southeast Asian refugees were truly uprooted. Lamented one of them, "They have no place they can call their own. They feel no sense of belonging to this land." In Texas, another refugee wrote:

> *In the obscurity of the night, a refugee cries*
> *His tear of woe flooded on his eyes*
> *He sobs for homeless life, the uncertainty of tomorrow.*

Still, these refugees from Southeast Asia, as well as the other Asian immigrants who have come to America since

1965, have been making their homes in the new land. By 1990, there were some 600,000 Vietnamese, 250,000 Laotians, and 150,000 Cambodians in the United States. They have struggled to learn Western ways while still striving to hold onto the heritages of their homelands. Many have started businesses and have sent their children to schools and universities. All of them have created new ethnic communities and have brought new economic life to cities such as Chicago, Los Angeles, Minneapolis–St. Paul, Providence, Oakland, Seattle, and San Jose.

Together, these recent Asian Americans have been helping to redefine America, to make its society more multicultural, with a richer diversity of ethnic cultures and communities. Linh Do, who was a child when her family left Vietnam in 1975, said, "Returning to Vietnam is not a choice. Now I'm American culturally. But the Vietnamese community in California has grown so large that you almost don't have to go home to be home. Here you can find Vietnamese food, dances, and culture."

"If Vietnam were a free country," said Loan Vo Le, who fled from Saigon in April 1975, "I would like to go back. I miss my family so much. But we couldn't stay. I'm afraid we are too spoiled by life here, the conveniences, the opportunities, and education and the freedom. . . . I feel like a Vietnamese American, but inside I'm still Vietnamese."

Chronology

1860s	France makes Vietnam a French colony.
1893	France colonizes Laos.
1939–45	World War II; Vietnamese nationalists fight against the French colonial forces.
1954	France withdraws from Indochina; Vietnam is divided into North and South Vietnam, which go to war with one another.
1960s	The United States enters the Vietnam War as the ally of South Vietnam.
1975	The Vietnam War ends in victory for North Vietnam; the first wave of Vietnamese refugees flees South Vietnam; refugees also begin leaving Laos after the communist takeover there; Pol Pot and the Khmer Rouge come to power in Cambodia.
1979	Vietnam invades Cambodia; the exodus of Cambodian refugees begins; an agreement between the United States and Vietnam allows Vietnamese to enter the United States as immigrants to join family members.
1979–80	Mien and Hmong refugees begin resettlement in the United States.
1979–82	The second wave of Vietnamese refugees, the "boat people," reaches North America.
1980s	The immigration of Amerasians begins.
1993	The United States and Vietnam resume trade relations.

Further Reading

The Boat People: An "Age" Investigation with Bruce Grant.
    New York: Penguin, 1979.

Chung, Hoang Chuong, and Van Le, Chung. *The Amerasians from Vietnam: A California Study.* Folsom, CA: Southeast Asia Community Resource Center, 1994.

Fawcett, James T., and Benjamin Carino. *Pacific Bridges: The New Immigrants from Asia and the Pacific Isles.* Staten Island, NY: Center for Migration Studies, 1987.

Fiffer, Sharon Sloan. *Imagining America: Paul Thai's Journey from the Killing Fields of Cambodia to Freedom in the U.S.A.* New York: Paragon, 1991.

Freeman, James M. *Hearts of Sorrow: Vietnamese-American Lives.* Stanford, CA: Stanford University Press, 1989.

Gogol, Sara. *Vatsana's Lucky New Year.* Minneapolis: Lerner Publications, 1992.

Hamilton-Merritt, Jane. *Tragic Mountains: The Hmong, the Americans, and the Secret Wars for Laos, 1942–1992.* Bloomington: Indiana University Press, 1993.

Hayslip, Le Ly. *Child of War, Woman of Peace.* New York: Doubleday, 1993.

Howard, Katsuyo K. *Passages: An Anthology of the Southeast Asian Refugee Experience.* Fresno: California State University, 1990.

Huynk, Jade Ngoc Quang. *South Wind Changing.* St. Paul, MN: Graywolf Press, 1994.

Knoll, Tricia. *Becoming American: Asian Sojourners, Immigrants, and Refugees in the Western United States.* Portland, OR: Coast to Coast, 1982.

Liu, William T. *Transition to Nowhere: Vietnamese Refugees in America.* Nashville, TN: Pacific-Asian American Mental Health Research Center, 1979.

Matthews, Ellen. *Culture Clash.* Chicago: Intercultural Press, 1982.

May, Someth. *Cambodian Witness: The Autobiography of Someth May.* New York: Random House, 1987.

Ngor, Haing, with Roger Warner. *Cambodian Odyssey.* New York: Macmillan, 1987.

Nguyen-Hong-Nhiem, Lucy, and Joel M. Halpern, eds. *The East Comes Near: Autobiographical Accounts of Southeast Asian Students in America.* Amherst: University of Massachusetts Press, 1989.

O'Connor, Karen. *Dan Thuy's New Life in America.* Minneapolis: Lerner Publications, 1992.

Rutledge, Paul. *The Vietnamese Experience in America.* Bloomington: Indiana University Press, 1992.

———— *The Vietnamese in America.* Minneapolis: Lerner Publications, 1987.

Stanek, Muriel. *We Come from Vietnam.* Niles, IL: Whitman, 1985.

Szymusiak, Molyda. *The Stones Cry Out: A Cambodian Childhood, 1975–1980.* Translated by Linda Coverdale. New York: Hill & Wang, 1986.

Tenhula, John. *Voices from Southeast Asia: The Refugee Experience in the United States.* New York: Holmes & Meier, 1991.

Wain, Barry. *The Refused: The Agony of the Indochina Refugees.* New York: Simon and Schuster, 1982.

Index

RONALD TAKAKI, the son of immigrant plantation laborers from Japan, graduated from the College of Wooster, Ohio, and earned his Ph.D. in history from the University of California at Berkeley, where he has served both as the chairperson and the graduate adviser of the Ethnic Studies program. Professor Takaki has lectured widely on issues relating to ethnic studies and multiculturalism in the United States, Japan, and the former Soviet Union and has won several important awards for his teaching efforts. He is the author of six books, including the highly acclaimed *Strangers from a Different Shore: A History of Asian Americans,* and the recently published *A Different Mirror: A History of Multicultural America.*

REBECCA STEFOFF is a writer and editor who has published more than 50 nonfiction books for young adults. Many of her books deal with geography and exploration, including the three-volume set *Extraordinary Explorers,* recently published by Oxford University Press. Stefoff also takes an active interest in environmental issues. She served as editorial director for two Chelsea House series—*Peoples and Places of the World* and *Let's Discover Canada.* Stefoff studied English at the University of Pennsylvania, where she taught for three years. She lives in Portland, Oregon.